The Effects of Sediment and Mercury Mobilization in the South Yuba River and Humbug Creek Confluence Area, Nevada County, California: Concentrations, Speciation, and Environmental Fate—Part 2: Laboratory Experiments

Mark Marvin-DiPasquale, Jennifer L. Agee, Evangelos Kakouros, Le H. Kieu, Jacob A. Fleck, and Charles N. Alpers

Prepared in cooperation with the
Bureau of Land Management and the
California State Water Resources Control Board

Open-File Report 2010–1325B

U.S. Department of the Interior
U.S. Geological Survey

U.S. Department of the Interior
KEN SALAZAR, Secretary

U.S. Geological Survey
Marcia K. McNutt, Director

U.S. Geological Survey, Reston, Virginia: 2011

For more information on the USGS—the Federal source for science about the Earth,
its natural and living resources, natural hazards, and the environment,
visit http://www.usgs.gov or call 1–888–ASK–USGS.

For an overview of USGS information products, including maps, imagery, and publications,
visit http://www.usgs.gov/pubprod

To order this and other USGS information products, visit http://store.usgs.gov

Suggested citation:
Marvin-DiPasquale, M., Agee, J.L., Kakouros, E., Kieu, L.H., Fleck, J.A., and Alpers, C.N.,
2011, The effects of sediment and mercury mobilization in the South Yuba River and Humbug
Creek confluence area, Nevada County, California: Concentrations, speciation and
environmental fate—Part 2: Laboratory Experiments: U.S. Geological Survey Open-File
Report 2010–1325B; 54 p.

Contents

Figures

Tables

Conversion Factors

Inch/Pound to SI

Multiply	By	To obtain
Length		
inch (in.)	2.54	centimeter (cm)
inch (in.)	25.4	millimeter (mm)
foot (ft)	0.3048	meter (m)
mile (mi)	1.609	kilometer (km)
yard (yd)	0.9144	meter (m)
Area		
square foot (ft^2)	929.0	square centimeter (cm^2)
square foot (ft^2)	0.09290	square meter (m^2)
square inch (in^2)	6.452	square centimeter (cm^2)
Volume		
ounce, fluid (fl. oz)	0.02957	liter (L)
pint (pt)	0.4732	liter (L)
quart (qt)	0.9464	liter (L)
gallon (gal)	3.785	liter (L)
cubic inch (in^3)	16.39	cubic centimeter (cm^3)
cubic inch (in^3)	0.01639	liter (L)
Flow rate		
gallon per day (gal/d)	0.003785	cubic meter per day (m^3/d)
Mass		
ounce, avoirdupois (oz)	28.35	gram (g)
pound, avoirdupois (lb)	0.4536	kilogram (kg)
ton per day (ton/d)	0.9072	metric ton per day
Density		
pound per cubic foot (lb/ft^3)	0.01602	gram per cubic centimeter (g/cm^3)

Temperature in degrees Celsius (°C) may be converted to degrees Fahrenheit (°F) as follows: °F=(1.8×°C)+32

Temperature in degrees Fahrenheit (°F) may be converted to degrees Celsius (°C) as follows: °C=(°F-32)/1.8

Concentrations of chemical constituents in water are given either in milligrams per liter (mg/L; parts per million, ppm), micrograms per liter (µg/L; parts per billion ppb), or nanograms per liter (ng/L; parts per trillion, ppt).

Acronyms, Abbreviations, and Chemical Notation

Acronyms

ANOVA, analysis of variance

BRC-P2, Bedrock contact layer–Pit 2, sampling location

DI, deionized (water)

DMW, Delta Meadows wetland

ENG, Englebright Lake (reservoir)

HMD, hydraulic mining debris

HMD-CF, hydraulic mining debris – cliff face, sampling location

ICP-MS, inductive coupled plasma mass spectrometry

K_{meth}, mercury methylation rate constant

LOI, loss on ignition

MPP, methymercury production potential

QA, quality assurance

RPDEV, relative percent deviation

RPSD, relative percent standard deviation

SFB, San Francisco Bay

TRS, total reduced sulfur

SYR-HC, South Yuba River–Humbug Creek

SYR-MC, South Yuba River–main channel

SYR-P1, South Yuba River–Pit 1, sampling location

USEPA, U.S. Environmental Protection Agency

USGS, U.S. Geological Survey

Abbreviations

cm, centimeter

cm^3, cubic centimeter

g, gram

in., inch

km, kilometer

L, liter

m, meter

mg, milligram

mg/g, milligram per gram (equivalent to part per thousand)

mg/kg, milligram per kilogram (equivalent to part per million)

mg/L, milligram per liter

mL, milliliter

mL/min, milliliter per minute

mV, millivolt

N, normality

ng, nanogram

ng/g, nanogram per gram (equivalent to part per billion

ng/L, nanogram per liter (equivalent to part per trillion

nmol/mL, nanomole per milliliter

pg, picogram

ppb, part per billion

ppm, part per million

µg, microgram

µg/g, microgram per gram (equivalent to part per million

µg/mL, microgram per milliliter (equivalent to milligram per liter

µm, micrometer

wt, weight

w/v, weight to volume

<, less than

%, percent

Chemical Notation

Au, gold

BrCl, bromine monochloride

CH_3Hg, methylmercury (monomethylmercury)

CH_3OH, methanol

$CrCl_3$, chromium(III) chloride

Fe, iron

$Fe(II)_{AE}$, acid extractable ferrous iron

$Fe(III)_a$, amorphous (poorly crystalline) ferric iron

$Fe(III)_c$, crystalline ferric iron

$FeSO_4$, ferrous sulfate

Fe_2O_3, magnetite

Fe_T, total measured iron ($Fe(II)_{AE} + Fe(III)_a + Fe(III)_c$)

HCl, hydrochloric acid

Hg, mercury

Hg(0), elemental mercury

Hg(II), (divalent) mercuric ion

$Hg(II)_R$, inorganic (divalent) reactive mercury

HgAu, mercury-gold amalgam

$HgCl_2$, mercuric chloride

Hg_2Cl_2, mercurous chloride (calomel)

HgS, mercury sulfide (cinnabar)

β-HgS, metacinnabar

$HgSO_4$, mercuric sulfate

HNO_3, nitric acid

KOH, potassium hydroxide

MeHg, methylmercury (monomethylmercury)

MeHgCl, methylmercury chloride

N_2, dinitrogen gas

Na_2S, sodium sulfide

O_2, dioxygen gas

$SnCl_2$, stannous chloride

THg, total mercury

ZnS, zinc sulfide

The Effects of Sediment and Mercury Mobilization in the South Yuba River and Humbug Creek Confluence Area, Nevada County, California: Concentrations, Speciation, and Environmental Fate—Part 2: Laboratory Experiments

Mark Marvin-DiPasquale[1], Jennifer L. Agee[1], Evangelos Kakouros[1], Le H. Kieu[1], Jacob A. Fleck[2], and Charles N. Alpers[2]

[1] U.S. Geological Survey, Branch of Regional Research, Western Region, 345 Middlefield Rd., Menlo Park, CA 94025

[2] U.S. Geological Survey, California Water Science Center, Placer Hall, 6000 J Street, Sacramento, CA 95819

Executive Summary

The South Yuba River (SYR), located on the western portion of the Sierra Nevada in California, is highly contaminated with mercury (Hg) as a result of historical gold (Au) mining that took place throughout this region starting in the mid 1800s and continuing into the early 1900s. During this period, the hydraulic mining of alluvial Au deposits formed during the Tertiary period (65.5 to 2.6 million years before present) was responsible for mobilizing hundreds of millions of tons of hydraulic mining debris (HMD), which was and continues to be redeposited in the SYR, its tributaries, and the San Francisco Bay Delta. Hydraulic mining was used in combination with the mercury-gold (Hg-Au) amalgamation process. Elemental mercury (Hg(0)) was introduced into Au recovery sluices to trap Au flakes, which were mixed with the sediment-water slurry produced from the hydraulic mobilization of sediment. As a result of inefficient trapping, some amount of both Hg(0) and Hg-Au amalgam was lost in this process. And along with the HMD, both can still be found throughout the SYR watershed, downstream of the major historic mining areas.

Today, there is concern about the level of Hg bioaccumulation in the SYR watershed and similarly affected former Au-mining locations throughout the Sierra Nevada. Further, Hg-contaminated HMD and sub-aqueous Hg-contaminated sediment can be remobilized both by natural processes and human activities, including recreational suction dredging. Thus, resource managers, anglers, and other watershed stakeholders are concerned that remobilizing Hg-contaminated sediment and HMD may exacerbate Hg bioaccumulation in downstream environments.

1

To address the above concerns, a study was conducted to assess the potential effects of recreational suction dredging in terms of 1) its viability as an approach to clean up riverbed sediment contaminated with legacy Hg from historical Au-mining activity, and 2) its effects on Hg remobilization, speciation (chemical form), and the potential for the stimulation of toxic methylmercury (MeHg) production and bioaccumulation in downstream environments. As part of this larger study, a series of laboratory experiments were conducted with various types of sediment material collected in and around the South Yuba River–Humbug Creek (SYR-HC) confluence area. This report describes the results of these laboratory experiments.

The experiments were conducted in three rounds (Experiments #1, #2, and #3), each with two parts (Part A and Part B). The three rounds of experiments differed largely in when they were conducted (separated by weeks to months) and what sediment or combination of sediment was studied. The two experimental parts in each round examined changes in Hg speciation as a result of sediment remobilization (Part A) and the capacity of remobilized sediment to stimulate MeHg production in downstream environments (Part B). A third study component (Part C) was added to Experiment #3, in which sequential extraction was used to assess the chemical composition of the various sediment material used in Parts A and B of Experiment #3.

The sediment material used in these laboratory studies was collected from three zones in and around the SYR-HC confluence area: a) hydraulic mining debris associated with an eroding cliff face (HMD-CF), b) hand-evacuated Pit #1 in a gravel bar located in the main channel of the South Yuba River (SYR-P1), and c) the bedrock contact layer associated with hand-evacuated Pit #2 (BRC-P2) located at the mouth of Humbug Creek. These three zones represented a 30-fold range in total mercury (THg) concentration ($\approx$ 0.3 to 11 milligrams per kilogram (mg/kg, or parts per million, ppm) and a wide range of geochemical compositions (for example, iron and sulfur speciation, organic content). All were selected because the sediment they contain is potentially subject to remobilization by natural erosion, high-flow runoff conditions, and (or) recreational suction dredging. Sediment collected from HMD-CF represents naturally eroding material and had a THg concentration of 1.40 ppm in the less than (<) 63 μm (silt-clay) size fraction. Sediment collected from SYR-P1 represents material likely to be remobilized during a natural high-flow event, or during removal of "overburden" during suction dredging, and had a THg concentration of 0.26 ppm in the <63 μm fraction. Sediment collected from BRC-P2 represents the desired dredging target or 'pay layer' with visible Au and had a THg concentration of 3.01 ppm in the 63–250 μm (fine sand) size fraction and 10.8 ppm in the <63 μm size fraction.

Part A of each experiment examined changes in Hg speciation associated with sediment mobilization under controlled conditions and demonstrated that Hg reactivity can increase when previously buried sediment is mobilized into an oxic overlying water column. Sediment mobilization simulations were carried out by combining filtered (0.22 μm) sterilized SYR water with the four sediment materials described above. Sediment-water slurries were stirred continuously while being purged with either air (oxic treatment) or dinitrogen (N$_2$) gas (anoxic treatment). The oxic treatment simulated natural conditions of transport in a typical, well-oxygenated river environment, whereas the anoxic treatment served as a control to assess the effect of water-column dissolved oxygen on Hg speciation. Slurry sub-samples were collected multiple times over a 6 to 8 day time course and assayed for inorganic 'reactive' mercury ($Hg(II)_R$), which is a methodologically defined surrogate measure of the fraction of THg that is most readily converted to MeHg by microbes.

For all four sediment materials tested, slurry $Hg(II)_R$ concentrations were greater under oxic conditions than under anoxic conditions during all or most of the time course. At the termination of each time-course experiment, the solid-phase material was recovered from the slurry flask and evaluated for the percentage of THg that occurred as $Hg(II)_R$ (expressed as $\%Hg(II)_R$). Solid-phase material from the oxic treatment typically had higher $\%Hg(II)_R$ than did material from the anoxic treatment. The one exception to this trend was the HMD-CF material, which there was no measurable difference from $\%Hg(II)_R$ between oxic and anoxic treatments for the post-slurry recovered solids.

The $Hg(II)_R$ concentration in the 63–250 µm BRC-P2 material was 4-fold higher in the post-slurry material (1.2–1.3 ppm) compared to the pre-slurry sediment (0.3 ppm). This same substrate and size fraction (BRC-P2, 63–250 µm) showed a similar 4-fold increase in $Hg(II)_R$ concentration when oven dried at 70°C for 48 hrs. The other materials tested (all <63 µm) did not show similar increases in $Hg(II)_R$ concentration under either slurry or oven-drying treatment conditions. MeHg concentrations associated with the HMD-CF (<63 µm) material were also higher in the post-slurry recovered solids (2.8 nanograms per gram (ng/g, or parts per billion, ppb) in the oxic treatment and 4.4 ppb in the anoxic treatment), compared to the pre-slurry concentration (1.4 ppb). This suggests that abiotic or microbial MeHg production occurred in the flasks containing the HMD-CF material during the week-long mobilization simulation. Similar evidence of MeHg production was not seen for either the SYR-P1 or the BRC-P2 material during the slurry experiments.

Part B experiments simulated what might happen with respect to MeHg concentrations when sediment material from the hydraulic mining-affected SYR-HC area is mobilized and then redeposited downstream. A small quantity of post-slurry solid-phase material (the 'spiking' sediment), pre-conditioned in Part A (under either oxic or anoxic conditions), was mixed with a larger quantity of 'receiving' sediment from various downstream environments (at a ratio of either 1:50 or 1:100 sediment wet weight), and net MeHg production was assessed after 1 week of incubation. The receiving sediment studied represented typical deposition zones where mobilized fine-grained sediment could eventually fall out and included material collected from the South Yuba River main channel (SYR-MC); Englebright Lake (ENG), a deep downstream reservoir; and Delta Meadows wetland (DMW), a shallow vegetated wetland site in the San Francisco Bay (SFB) Delta.

The results indicate that, depending on both the spiking and receiving sediment used, MeHg production could be stimulated in these mixed-sediment treatments compared to non-spiked receiving sediment controls. Although many combinations of 'spiking' and 'receiving' sediment were tested, the most pronounced results were seen when ENG and DMW sediment was spiked with BRC-P2 material. In these cases, MeHg concentration at the end of the incubation period was approximately 2-fold (ENG) to more than 3-fold (DMW) greater in the samples receiving the 'spiking' material, compared to their respective non-spiked controls. For a given receiving sediment, there was no apparent difference in the amount of MeHg produced based upon the pre-incubation treatment of the spiking material (oxic or anoxic) in Part A. At the end of the week-long incubation period, approximately 3 to 8% of the $Hg(II)_R$ associated with the BRC-P2 spiking material had been converted to MeHg, suggesting that a longer incubation period may have produced even greater MeHg concentrations. Statistically significant MeHg formation was also observed in the spike amended samples preserved on Day=0 (flash frozen soon after the spike addition), a result indicative of abiotic MeHg formation. Again, this was most pronounced with the BRC-P2 spiking material, which had a substantially greater $Hg(II)_R$ concentration compared to the SYR-P1 and HMD-CF spiking materials.

Part C experiments involved the sequential extraction analysis of HMD-CF, SYR-P1, and BRC-P2 material (all <63 μm). This experiment was designed to examine the relative composition of the three materials with respect to five chemically defined fractions (F1 thru F5, ranging from easily extractable (F1) to highly recalcitrant (F5)), with the goal of better interpreting the results obtained in Experiment #3, Parts A and B. The results indicate that the BRC-P2 material had higher proportions and absolute concentrations of Hg in the extracted fractions associated with elemental mercury (Hg(0), F4 fraction [12 M nitric acid extractable], 72% of THg) and Hg-Au amalgam (F5 fraction [aqua regia extractable], 24% of THg), compared to SYR-P1 and HMD-CF material. Part C results also suggest that in the sediment layers targeted by suction dredging enthusiasts (for example, BRC-P2), very fine-grained particles (<63 μm) that are typically not trapped in the sluice box and instead are transported downstream can contain a substantial amount of Hg, including elemental Hg(0) and Hg-Au amalgam.

Overall, the laboratory experiments demonstrate that potentially mobilized fine-grained sediment from the SYR-HC confluence exhibits a range of changes with respect to Hg speciation when subjected to laboratory conditions that simulate mobilization, transport, and deposition in a field setting. The nature and degree of changes in Hg speciation depend on the source material, its geochemical composition, and its particle-size distribution. The observed changes include an increase in $Hg(II)_R$ and (or) MeHg concentration of suspended particles. Sediment mixing experiments demonstrated that mobilization of very small amounts of fine-grained sediment enriched in $Hg(II)_R$ will stimulate MeHg production in receiving sediment typical of that downstream from historic hydraulic mining sites, including reservoirs and wetlands. Although the consequences of using suction dredging to remediate a Hg hotspot was not directly tested as part of the current set of laboratory experiments, the results of the simulation experiments presented here do provide some insight into this question as it pertains to the fate and transport of fine Hg-rich particles.

Introduction

The mobilization of previously deposited sediment is important with respect to contaminant transport, especially in watersheds affected by California's historic mining legacy. Because millions of tons of sediment were mobilized and contaminated with mercury (Hg) as a result of hydraulic gold (Au) mining in the Sierra Nevada and Klamath-Trinity Mountains (Alpers and others, 2005), contemporary sediment remobilization has the potential to reintroduce legacy contaminants, such as Hg, to the environment. There is a two-fold concern regarding the remobilization of Hg-contaminated sediment: 1) the disturbance and physical transport of sediment may alter the chemical speciation of the Hg associated with it, thus creating a more chemically reactive form of Hg, and 2) the remobilized Hg, now more reactive, may be redeposited in sensitive habitats where it may be further transformed into more bioavailable species (for example, methylmercury (MeHg)), and thereby increase the threat to wildlife and human health.

Numerous mechanisms can affect sediment remobilization. Previously deposited sediment can be mobilized naturally, due to an increase in the shear stress on bed sediment in response to changes in surface-water flow, such as those associated with spring snowmelt and seasonal rainy periods (Mount, 1995). Sediment can also be remobilized because of human activities, such as the dredging of navigation channels and streambed gravel mining, which are designed to either remove or otherwise relocate sediment. In addition, dam or levee construction that redirects hydrologic flow can affect the previous distribution of sediment scour and deposition zones and result in bed-sediment remobilization.

One human-induced sediment-mobilization practice of particular interest is suction dredging, a popular hobby activity used to reclaim Au from historic mining areas and from locations naturally enriched in Au, such as alluvial deposits in streams and rivers. Because elemental mercury (Hg(0)) was used to amalgamate Au in historic mining operations (Alpers and others, 2005), popular areas for recreational suction dredging are commonly contaminated with legacy Hg.

A typical contemporary suction dredge can be operated by a single person and consists of a vacuum hose (ranging from 2 to 10 in. in diameter) controlled by a scuba diver. The suction through the hose is provided by a motorized pump mounted to a floating pontoon that also houses an inclined sluice box. The sediment and water slurry is delivered from the suction hose, by the pump, to the top of the sluice box. As the slurry washes down the incline, the higher density particles of Au, Hg(0), and Hg-Au amalgam are trapped within the sluice box, while the lighter material (cobble, sand, silt, and clay) is ejected from the bottom of the box and back into the river. The suction dredging process is very effective at moving large quantities of riverbed sediment and exposing historically deposited sediment layers that would otherwise not be susceptible to erosion and remobilization during typical seasonal and episodic runoff events. Thus, an environmental concern with suction dredging is that the practice often targets Au-containing (and Hg-contaminated) sediment layers that otherwise are largely inaccessible to natural remobilization processes except during extreme conditions.

Although the direct influence of sediment remobilization may affect a reach of river in a number of ways, the greatest potential threat to wildlife and human health may occur after the remobilization event has long passed in both space and time, particularly in the case of deeply buried sediment. For example, in Alviso Slough, located in South San Francisco Bay, the simulated disturbance of previously buried Hg-bearing sediment was shown to cause a substantial increase in the inorganic (divalent) reactive mercury ($Hg(II)_R$) concentration under both oxic and anoxic laboratory conditions (Marvin-DiPasquale and Cox, 2007). Because $Hg(II)_R$ has been used as a surrogate measure of the divalent mercuric ion (Hg(II)) available to bacteria for Hg(II)-methylation (Marvin-DiPasquale and others, 2009a), these earlier studies suggest that there is a potential for increased MeHg productions from Hg(II) at downstream locations (for example, streambeds, reservoirs, or wetlands). This could ultimately result in enhanced threat of MeHg bioaccumulation in the food web.

Because the mechanisms associated with increased Hg reactivity and MeHg production likely occur post-remobilization, either *en route* to or following sediment redeposition in an unspecified downstream environment, it is impractical to document such mechanisms within a typical field study design. The use of laboratory controlled simulation experiments is therefore crucial to improve our understanding of the scale and extent of these processes, and the results from such experiments have transfer value to watersheds throughout the Sierra Nevada and other regions affected by hydraulic mining.

Purpose and Scope

This report documents methods and results from a series of laboratory experiments designed to examine various aspects of sediment-Hg remobilization using a range of sediment types collected from multiple habitats associated with the South Yuba River–Humbug Creek (SYR-HC) confluence area. The specific goals of these experiments were two-fold: 1) to evaluate how simulated sediment mobilization may affect Hg speciation, with particular emphasis on $Hg(II)_R$ concentration, and 2) to determine whether particulate material from the mobilization experiments could lead to increased MeHg production when mixed with sediment from three downstream environmental settings where mobilized fine-grained silt-clay may be ultimately redeposited.

Resource agencies and other stakeholders are interested in evaluating Hg in this watershed because Humbug Creek is the drainage outlet of Malakoff Diggins, the largest historical hydraulic mining operation in the northern Sierra Nevada (see Fleck and others, 2011 and references therein). The experiments presented in this report were coordinated with a field study that characterized the distribution and speciation of Hg in sediment, water, and biota in and around the SYR-HC confluence area (Fleck and others, 2011). This combined field and laboratory investigation was designed to evaluate the environmental effects of suction dredging, which has been proposed as a potential cleanup technique for Hg-contaminated sediments at the SYR-HC confluence and other remote sites contaminated by historical Au mining operations. The results presented here provide a scientific basis for understanding the potential environmental effects of Hg remobilization and (or) removal by a standard suction dredge.

Methods

Laboratory Experiments: Overview

Three rounds of laboratory experiments (Experiments #1, #2, and #3) were conducted, each with two parts (Part A and Part B). The distinction between the three experiments was that they were conducted at different times (separated by weeks to months) and examined different types of sediment or sediment combinations (table 1). However, the general design of each of the three experiments was essentially the same. Part A of each experiment was a sediment-mobilization simulation designed to track changes in $Hg(II)_R$ concentration over 1 week, in a slurry created from mixing previously buried sediment with filtered sterilized river water, while continuously stirring and gassing under either oxic or anoxic conditions. Part B of each experiment was a sediment mixing / MeHg production study, in which a small amount of the material pre-conditioned in Part A was used as the 'spiking' sediment and was added to a larger amount of an unique 'receiving sediment.' After a week of incubation, the subsequent production of MeHg was then assessed in each spiking / receiving sediment mixed treatment.

Table 1. Summary of Experiments #1 through #3.

[The sediment type and size fraction used for each of the three experiments are shown. Each experiment had two parts. Part A represents the sediment mobilization simulation (reactive mercury time course) experiment and included both oxic and anoxic slurry conditions. Part B represents the sediment mixing experiment where the solid-phase material collected from Part A (after the slurry preconditioning step) was added to various 'receiving' sediment. The Spike Ratio details the 'spiking sediment' (from Part A) to 'receiving sediment' ratio given in grams (g/g) wet weight. **Abbreviations:** BRC-P2, bedrock contact layer from Pit 2; SYR-MC, South Yuba River–main channel bed sediment; SYR-P1, South Yuba River–Pit 1, HMD-CF, Hydraulic mining debris from the eroding cliff face; ENG, Englebright Lake (reservoir); DMW, Delta Meadows wetland; µm, micrometer]

Experiment	Part A: Sediment used, size fraction (Spiking sediment used for Part B)	Part B: Receiving sediment used, size fraction	Part B: Spike ratio (g/g)
#1	BRC-P2, 63–250 µm	SYR-MC, <1,000 µm	(0.1/10) = 1:100
#2	BRC-P2, <63 µm	SYR-P1, <63 µm	(0.1/10) = 1:100
#3	SYR-P1, <63 µm	ENG, non-sieved silt/clay	(0.1/5) = 1:50
#3	SYR-P1, <63 µm	DMW, non-sieved silt/clay	(0.1/5) = 1:50
#3	HMD-CF, <63 µm	ENG, non-sieved silt/clay	(0.1/5) = 1:50
#3	HMD-CF, <63 µm	DMW, non-sieved silt/clay	(0.1/5) = 1:50
#3	BRC-P2, <63 µm	ENG, non-sieved silt/clay	(0.1/5) = 1:50
#3	BRC-P2, <63 µm	DMW, non-sieved silt/clay	(0.1/5) = 1:50

A third study component (Part C) was added to Experiment #3, in which sequential extraction was used to assess the chemical composition of the various sediment material used in Parts A and B of Experiment #3, with respect to five chemically defined fractions (F1 thru F5, ranging from easily extractable (F1) to highly recalcitrant (F5)). The goal of Part C was to obtain more detailed Hg-speciation data and to use this information to more fully interpret the results obtained in Experiment #3, Parts A and B.

Field Collection

Sediment and river water used in laboratory Experiments #1, #2, and #3, Part A (sediment-mobilization simulation) (table 1), were collected from the SYR-HC confluence area (figs. 1 and 2) during September 2008 in conjunction with a related site characterization study (Fleck and others, 2011). The sediment was hand-evacuated and sieved into three size fractions:

(1) Coarse to medium sand, 0.25 to 1.0 mm (250 to 1,000 µm),

(2) Fine sand, 0.063 to 0.25 mm (63 to 250 µm), and

(3) Silt and clay, less than 0.063 mm (<63 µm).

The smallest size fraction (<63 μm) was transported from the field in stainless steel containers as a slurry mixture of the solid-phase particles and the river water that had been used to wet sieve the larger size fractions. In addition, river water from the SYR for use in the experiments was transported to the laboratory in similar stainless steel containers.

A subset of the sediment collected in the field was selected for the laboratory experiments (table 1) on the basis of the THg concentration (low to high range, 0.3 to 11 ppm) and the likelihood of mobilization by various natural and anthropogenic mechanisms, in such a way as to bookend the potential Hg effects on downstream environments. Upon returning from the field, all material was stored refrigerated at 5°C in the laboratory until further sub-sampling, as described below. The materials selected for Part A experiments included:

(1) South Yuba River material collected from Pit #1 (SYR-P1) located on a dry gravel bar in the river's main channel. Pit #1 was conical in shape and approximately 0.9 m deep at the center point. The material used in the laboratory experiments came from the processing of the full pit, after the top 0.15 m of overburden material (large cobble) was removed (see fig. 7 in Fleck and others, 2011).

(2) Bedrock contact material collected from Pit #2 (BRC-P2) located at the mouth of Humbug Creek. The depth of this layer varied (from approximately 0.5 to 2 m) depending on the bedrock slope, and there was no overlying surface water associated with Pit #2 at the time of sample collection (see fig. 9 in Fleck and others, 2011).

(3) Hydraulic mining debris collected from the eroding cliff face (HMD-CF). The material was dry at the time of collection. Four vertical channels (approximately 0.6–1.0 m in length, 15 cm wide, and 5 cm deep), spaced horizontally at approximately 7.5 m intervals over a 30 m horizontal section of the cliff face, were hand-evacuated. Taken together, the four vertical channels represent three vertical meters of the stratigraphic section, and approximately one-third of the vertical extent of the exposed cliff face (see fig. 10 in Fleck and others, 2011).

The 'receiving sediment' used in laboratory Experiments #1 and #2, Part B (MeHg production assay) (table 1), was also collected as part of the September 2008 site characterization (Fleck and others, 2011), and included:

(1) South Yuba River bed sediment collected from the main channel (SYR-MC). This material was collected from a sandy bar under approximately 10 cm of flowing surface water. The material was initially evacuated with a small shovel to a depth of approximately 10 cm.

(2) South Yuba River material collected from Pit #1 (SYR-P1), as described above.

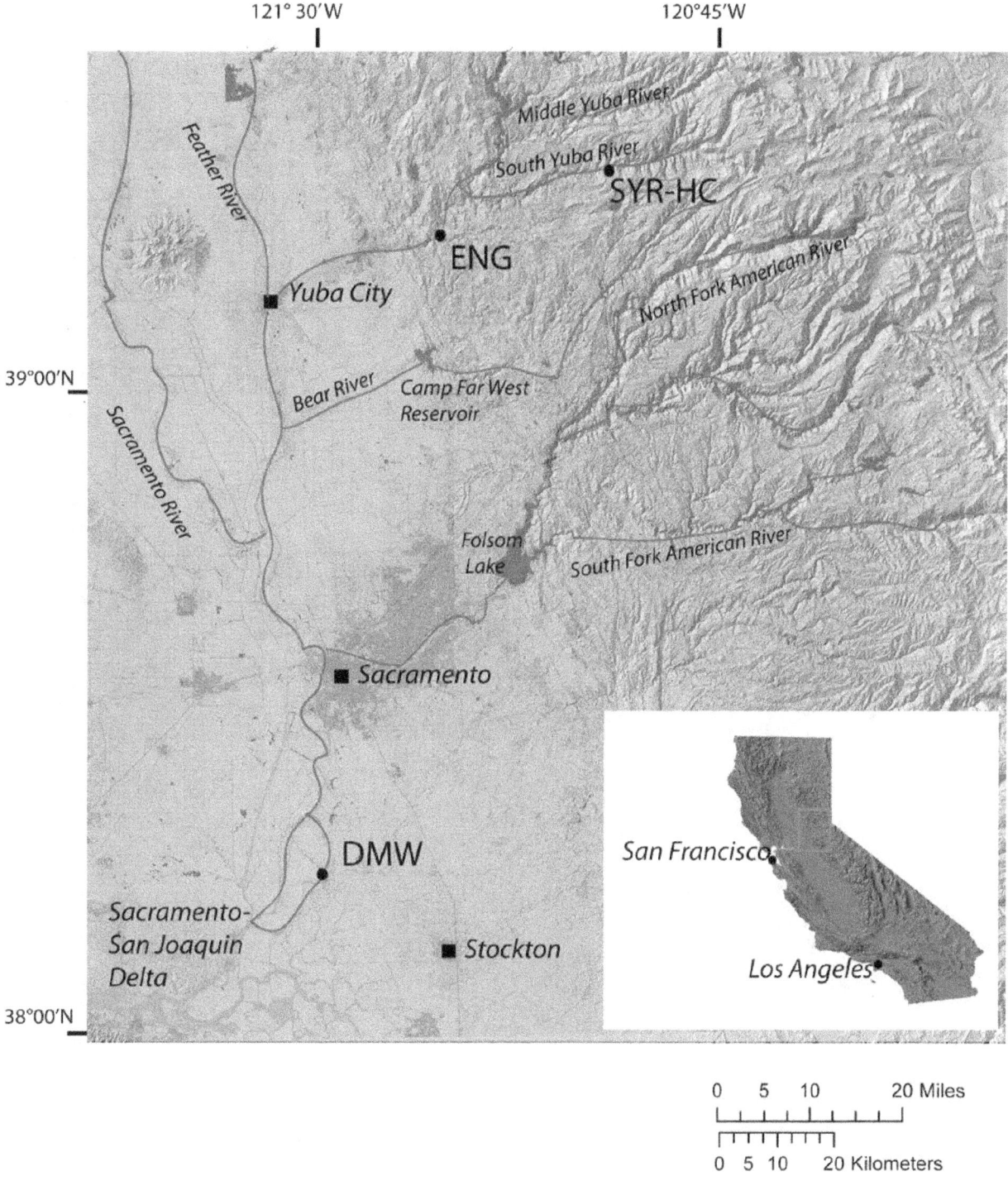

Figure 1. Map showing the location of the South Yuba River – Humbug Creek (SYR-HC) primary study area sampled during September 2008, and the locations of Englebright Lake (ENG) and Delta Meadows wetland (DMW) sampled for downstream 'receiving sediment' during July 2009. The red rectangle in the inset map of California identifies the location of the larger map within the state.

9

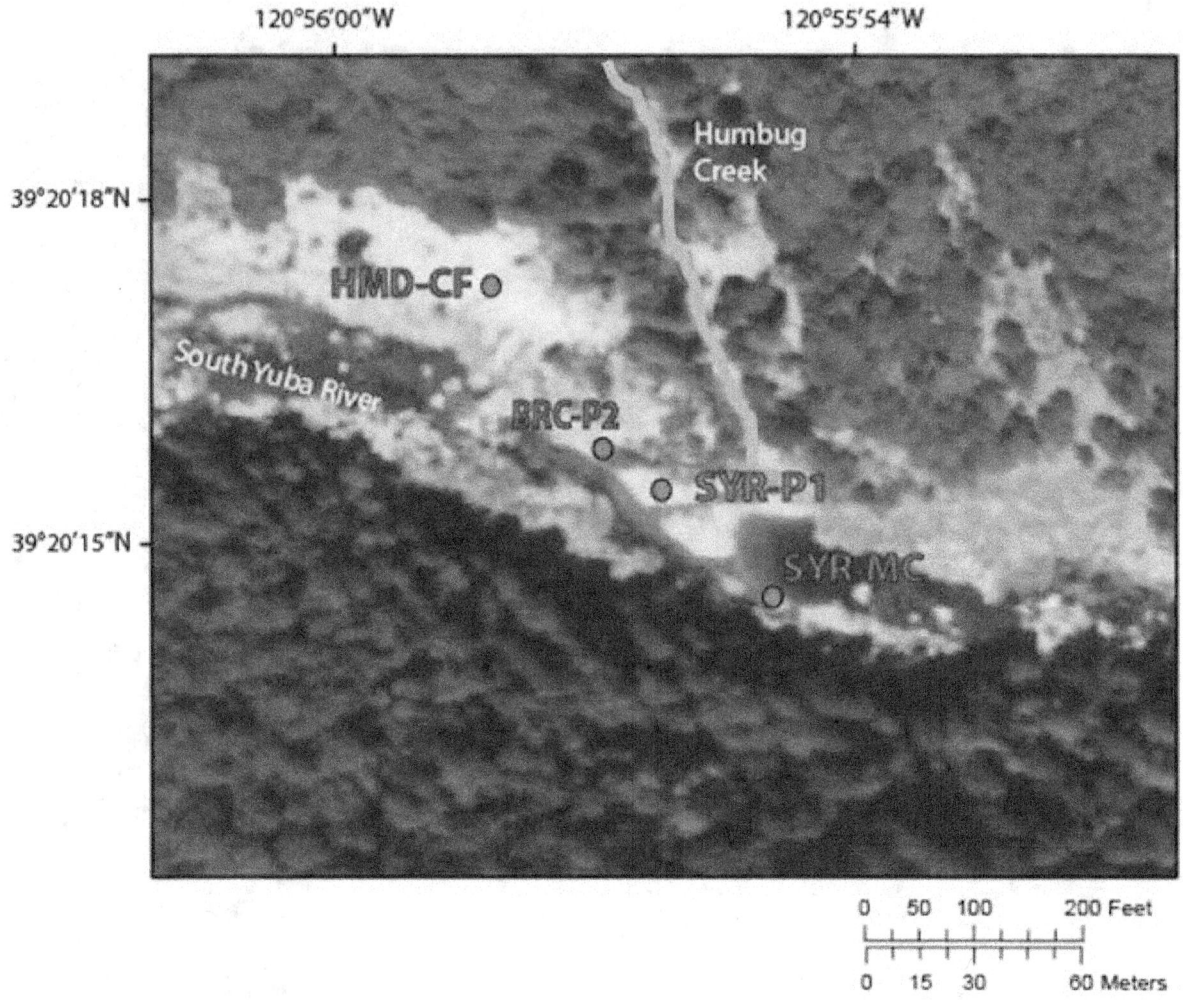

Figure 2. Satellite image showing the sediment sampling locations within the South Yuba River – Humbug Creek sampling area during September 2008; South Yuba River – Pit 1 (SYR-P1), South Yuba River – main channel (SYR-MC), hydraulic mining debris associated with the eroding cliff face (HMD-CF), and bedrock contact – Pit 2 (BRC-P2) at the mouth of Humbug Creek.

The receiving sediment used in Experiment #3, Part B (table 1), was collected during July 2009 from two sources downstream of the SYR-HC confluence area (fig. 1):

(1) Englebright Lake (ENG) is located approximately 42 river km downstream of SYR-HC. Sediment was sampled using an Eckman box core from a location in the reservoir approximately 0.7 km upstream from Englebright Dam [39°14'44.95"N, 121°16'7.29"W]. The overlying water depth was approximately 60 m. Surface sediment (top 0–2 cm) was then sampled from the box core using a polycarbonate ring that was 2 cm long (inner diameter of 6 cm) and then transferred into acid-cleaned mason jars. Sediment samples were stored chilled on wet ice during transit back to the laboratory and were subsequently stored refrigerated (5°C) until further sub-sampling the following day.

(2) Delta Meadows wetland (DMW) is an emergent wetland site located on California State Park land, approximately 112 km southwest of Englebright Dam (fig. 1), just east of the historic central-Delta town of Locke, CA [38°15'3.17"N, 121°30'17.94"W]. Surface sediment (top 0–2 cm) was sampled by hand in shallow overlying water (0.5 m) using a polycarbonate core ring that was 2 cm long (inner diameter of 6 cm) and was preserved as described above, until further sub-sampling the following day.

Pre-Experiment Sub-Sampling

Sediment used in Parts A and B of Experiments #1 and #2, and Part A of Experiment #3, was sub-sampled in the laboratory 5–7 days after field collection for the coarse-to-medium sand (250−1,000 μm) and fine sand (63–250 μm) size fractions. The solids in the <63 μm size fraction were isolated using centrifugation and were sub-sampled 40 to 57 days after field collection. During this sub-sampling phase, sediment was collected and preserved as described by Fleck and others (2011) for the following constituents: THg, $Hg(II)_R$, water content (% dry weight), bulk density, and organic content (as weight 'loss on ignition'; LOI). The receiving sediment used in Part B of Experiment #3 was similarly sub-sampled and preserved in the laboratory 1 day after field collection for the subsequent analysis of the above constituents, as well as for MeHg concentration, oxidation-reduction potential (E_h), pH, iron (Fe) speciation, total reduced sulfur (TRS), and MeHg production potential (MPP) via stable isotope incubation.

Experiments #1 thru #3, Part A: Sediment Mobilization Simulation and $Hg(II)_R$ Time Course

The mason jar containing the BRC-P2 fine sand fraction (63−250 μm) material used in Experiment #1, Part A, was left out on the laboratory bench at room temperature for 1 week prior to mixing sediment with river water. This pre-conditioning step was done to maximize the reducing conditions in the sediment, so as to mimic something akin to the original conditions prior to excavation, and thus to potentially decrease the $\%Hg(II)_R$ in the starting material prior to creating the suspended slurries.

The dissolved oxygen (O_2) content in the stainless steel canisters of water from the SYR (collected during September 2008 and stored at 5°C) was measured prior to filtration using a hand-held, self-calibrating dissolved O_2 meter (Wissenschaftlich-Technische Werkstätten, Model oxi 330, equipped with a CellOx 325 membrane probe), and was found to be 85–87% of saturation, indicating that the water had not gone anoxic during the 6-month holding period at 5°C. Four liters of river water were then filtered using pre-combusted glass-fiber filters (0.22 μm pore size), and the filtrate was collected in pre-combusted 1-L amber glass bottles.

Four gas-purging vessels were constructed using pre-combusted 1-L Erlenmeyer flasks fitted with a 3-hole black rubber stopper. One hole served as a vent (with a 1-cm^3 plastic syringe inserted), the second hole served as the gas-in line with a fritted glass gas diffusion rod adjusted to approximately 5–8 cm off the bottom of the flask; the third hole served as the sampling port, with a 3-way stopcock on the top side and a plastic tube on the inside of the flask situated about 8–10 cm off of the bottom. The four flasks were labeled as follows: oxic-A, oxic-B, anoxic-A, and anoxic-B, reflecting the two treatment conditions (air purged, oxic; N$_2$ gas purged, anoxic) in duplicate (A and B). Filtered river water (1 L) was then transferred into each of four flasks, and the exact mass of river water in each flask was measured by weight, from which volume was calculated assuming a density of 1.0 g/cm^3. Gas cylinders (either air or N$_2$) were connected to each of the flasks using plastic tubing, and the gas flow rate was set to 40–45 mL/min. The filtered river water in each flask was purged (pre-conditioned) for approximately 60 hrs and then sub-sampled for THg and Hg(II)$_R$ analyses (50 mL for each) prior to the addition of sediment.

Sediment from each mason jar was sub-sampled under anoxic conditions for analysis of THg and Hg(II)$_R$ concentrations before sediment was added to the water flasks. The Hg(II)$_R$ sub-samples (0.1–0.15 g) were preserved in 10 ml of 0.5% anoxic HCl, and both THg and Hg(II)$_R$ sediment sub-samples were flash frozen on dry ice and ethanol, and stored frozen (-80°C). Each flask was then sub-sampled for dissolved THg and Hg(II)$_R$ (50 mL for each) in filtered river water, prior to the addition of sediment. Approximately 5 g of sediment (exact weight noted) was then added to each flask, making an average final concentration of 6.0±0.2 g wet sediment per liter or 4.0±0.1 g dry sediment per liter, n=4). The flask contents were suspended by continuous stirring with a Teflon™ coated magnetic stir-bar and were purged continuously with either air (oxic treatments) or N$_2$ (anoxic treatments). After approximately 20 minutes of mixing, the Day=0 subsamples (9 mL of slurry; exact mass determined by weight) were collected in duplicate from each container via the 3-way port. The slurry sub-samples were assayed immediately for Hg(II)$_R$ (see below). Sub-samples for Hg(II)$_R$ were similarly collected and assayed on days 1, 2, 3, 4, 7, and 8 of the Part A experiments. Dissolved O$_2$ levels were monitored daily and were found to be between 2–6% of saturation in the N$_2$-purged flasks, with the exception of Day=1, when one of the two replicate samples had a dissolved O$_2$ level of 15%. The N$_2$ gas flow rate was therefore increased to 80 mL/min on Day=2 of the slurry experiment, resulting in consistently low dissolved O$_2$ levels for the remainder of the experiment. Dissolved O$_2$ levels in the air-purged flasks were between 91–101% of saturation.

At the end of the sediment-mobilization experiment (Day=8) after the last Hg(II)$_R$ sub-samples were collected, the slurry flasks were transferred to a N$_2$-flushed glove bag for further processing under anoxic conditions. The remaining slurry was transferred from each flask into acid-cleaned 250 mL plastic airtight centrifuge containers. The solid phase was separated from the liquid phase via centrifugation for 15 minutes at 4,000 revolutions per minute (rpm). The supernatant was decanted into a pre-combusted amber glass bottle and sub-sampled for THg and Hg(II)$_R$, the latter of which was assayed immediately (see below), whereas the former (THg) was preserved with HCl (final concentrations of 0.5% HCl). In a N$_2$-flushed glove bag, the solid-phase material was scraped out of the bottom of the centrifuge bottles and transferred into four pre-combusted serum vials corresponding to the original four slurry flask designations. The final mass of each composite was recorded, with approximately 5.5 g wet sediment recovered per flask. Triplicate sub-samples (about 0.7 g each) were collected from each of the four samples for determination of dry weight. The remaining material was stored frozen under anaerobic conditions overnight until the initiation of the Part B experiments (mixing and Hg(II)-methylation) the following day.

Experiment #2, Part A, was conducted in a very similar fashion to Experiment #1, Part A, with the following exceptions:

(1) BRC-P2 (<63 µm size fraction) sediment was used.

(2) The material was allowed to pre-incubate for 28 days in a filled mason jar at room temperature, to optimize initial sediment reducing conditions prior to creating the slurry.

(3) The average final slurry composition was 6.6±0.4 g wet sediment per liter, or 3.0±0.2 g dry sediment per liter, n=4).

(4) The continuous air flow rate was set to 50–55 mL/min and the N_2 gas flow rate was set to 80 mL/min. Dissolved O_2 levels were checked daily and were found to be between 2–5% of saturation in the N_2 flasks and between 92–96% of saturation in the air-purged flasks.

(5) Approximately 1–2 mL of slurry (exact mass determined by weight) was sub-sampled via the 3-way port in duplicate from each contai ner on days 0, 1, 2, 3, 4, 7, and 8.

Experiment #3, Part A, was conducted in a fashion similar to Experiments #1 and #2, Part A, with the following exceptions:

(1) Three sediment materials were tested simultaneously (SYR-P1, HMD-CF, and BRC-P2, all <63 µm size fraction).

(2) Sediment was allowed to pre-incubate in mason jars at room temperature for only 1 day prior to creating the slurry.

(3) The river water was allowed to precondition via air- or N_2-purging for approximately 16 hours prior to the addition of sediment.

(4) Sub-samples for analysis of TRS and Fe speciation were collected from each mason jar of sediment immediately prior to the addition of sediment to the slurry flask.

(5) Approximately 10 g of wet sediment was added to each slurry flask, resulting in a final slurry composition (in grams of dry sediment per liter, n=2 for each type) of SYR-P, 6.9±0.1; HMD-CF, 7.2±0.1; and BRC-P2, 5.7±0.0.

(6) Each material type was continuously purged under oxic (with air) or anoxic (with N_2) conditions with only one replicate flask per treatment (fig. 3).

(7) Slurry sub-samples for Hg(II)$_R$ were 10 mL for SYR-P1 flasks and 3–5 mL for both HMD-CF and BRC-P2 flasks and were sampled in duplicate from each container on days 0, 1, 2, 5, and 6.

(8) Dissolved O_2 was monitored daily throughout the time course and ranged from 97–101% of saturation in all oxic flasks and from 1–3% of saturation in all anoxic flasks.

(9) Slurry sub-samples for TRS and Fe-speciation analysis (5 mL each in duplicate) were collected at the beginning (Day=0) and the end (Day=6) of the continuous mixing/purging period.

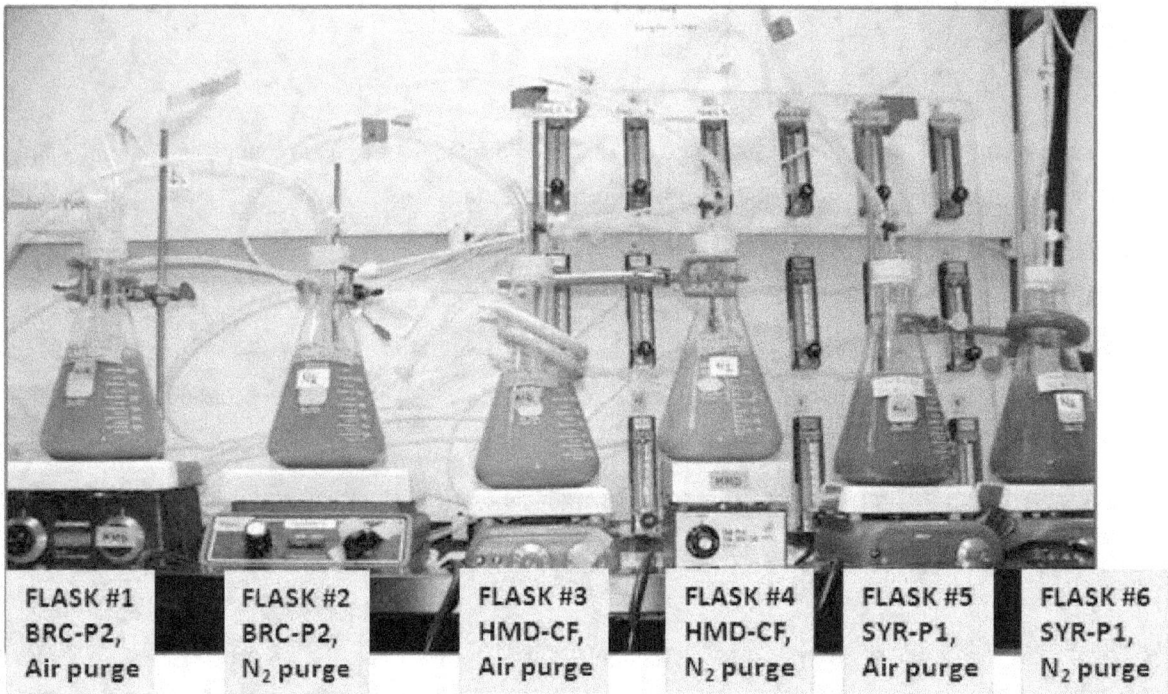

Figure 3. Photograph of the six flasks containing a slurry of sediment and river water associated with Experiment #3 Part A (reactive mercury time course). All sediment used in Experiment #3 was from the <63 μm size fraction and included Bedrock contact layer - Pit 2 (BRC-P2), hydraulic mining debris – cliff face (HMD-CF), and South Yuba River – Pit 1 (SYR-P1). Each flask was continuously purged with either air (oxic treatment) on nitrogen (N_2) gas (anoxic treatment) and stirred with a Teflon coated stir bar for 7 days.

Experiments #1 thru #3, Part B: Sediment Mixing Experiments / MeHg Production

Five days prior to the end of Experiment #1, Part A, the SYR-MC (<1 mm) sediment was sub-sampled (10.0±0.1 g) under anaerobic conditions into 13-cm^3 vials (40 vials in total) in preparation for its use as the receiving sediment in Experiment #1, Part B. The serum vials were then pre-incubated at room temperature for 6 days prior to the addition of the 'spiking' sediment, which represented the initiation of the Part B (sediment mixing / MeHg production) experiment.

After 6 days of pre-incubation and 1 day following the collection of the post-slurry material at the end of Experiment #1, Part A, the 40 serum vials containing the receiving sediment (SYR-MC, <1 mm) were randomized and labeled [treatment / time point / replicate] according to the following experimental design:

(1) Five treatments (one control, plus the four slurry flask designations from Part A: 'oxic A,' 'oxic B,' 'anoxic A,' and 'anoxic B'),

(2) Two time points for each treatment group (Day=0 and Day=7), and

(3) Four replicates (R1 through R4) for each treatment group / time-point combination.

The 40 receiving sediment vials and the post-slurry material collected from each of the four slurry flasks (Part A) were transferred into a N_2-flushed glove bag. Approximately 0.1 g of the pre-conditioned 'spiking' sediment from Part A (BRC-P2, 63–250 μm) was then added to the 10.0±0.1 g of receiving sediment in the serum vials, for a final amendment (wet mass) ratio (spike/receiving sediment) of 1:100. The complete transfer of the spiking sediment into the serum vial was facilitated by rinsing the small plastic weight boat (used to initially weigh the spiking sediment sub-sample) clean with 1.0 mL of anoxic deionized (DI) water delivered from a pneumatic pipette. The exact amount of spiking sediment transferred to each vial was determined by mass. The set of 'control' treatment vials did not receive any spiking sediment but did receive 1.0 mL of anoxic DI water in addition to receiving sediment. All samples were homogenized immediately after receiving the sediment spike and (or) the anoxic DI water. Half of the samples, those labeled Day=0, were placed in a -80°C freezer to arrest any subsequent production of MeHg. The remaining half of the samples (labeled Day=7) were placed in an incubator set for 21°C, and then similarly frozen after the 7 days had elapsed.

Experiment #2, Part B, was conducted in a fashion very similar to Experiment #1, Part B, with the following exception:

(1) The receiving sediment used was SYR-P1 (<63 μm).

Experiment #3, Part B, was conducted in a fashion very similar to Experiments #1 and #2, Part B, with the following exceptions:

(1) Three 'spiking' materials were tested simultaneously (SYR-P1, HMD-CF, and BRC-P2, all <63 μm size fraction),

(2) The receiving sediment used was from ENG and DMW, and

(3) The wet mass ratio of spike:receiving sediment was 1:50.

Experiment #3, Part C: Mercury Speciation by Sequential Extraction

As part of the characterization of the three 'spiking' materials used in Experiment #3 (SYR-P1, HMD-CF, and BRC-P2), a sequential extraction approach was used to determine Hg speciation (Bloom and others, 2003). This analysis consists of five sequentially extracted fractions of increasing strength (F1 thru F5). Each sediment type was assayed in triplicate and each extraction fraction was subsequently assayed for THg, according to U.S. Environmental Protection Agency (USEPA) Method 1631 Revision E (U.S. Environmental Protection Agency, 2002). A summary of the extractants used and the dominant Hg species associated with each fraction is given in table 2.

Table 2. Experiment #3, Part C—Sequential extraction experiment fractions and dominant mercury species.

[The mercury sequential extraction sequence, as per Bloom and others (2003), with each fraction number (F#) described by both the extraction solution used and the dominant mercury species associated with that fraction.
Abbreviations: DI, deionized; N, normality; HCl, hydrochloric acid; HNO_3, nitric acid; KOH, potassium hydroxide; Hg, mercury; $HgCl_2$, mercuric chloride; $HgSO_4$, mercuric sulfate; Hg(II), divalent inorganic mercury; CH_3Hg, methylmercury (i.e. MeHg); Hg(0), elemental mercury; Hg_2Cl_2, mercurous chloride, HgS, cinnabar; β-HgS, metacinnabar; HgAu, mercury-gold amalgam]

F# and extraction solution		Dominant Hg species
F1	DI water	Soluble; $HgCl_2$, $HgSO_4$
F2	pH=2; 0.1 N acetic acid + 0.01 N HCl	HgO, $HgSO_4$
F3	1 N KOH	Organic or particle-bound Hg(II); CH_3Hg; Hg_2Cl_2
F4	12 N HNO_3	elemental Hg(0); Hg_2Cl_2, HgAu
F5	Aqua regia (HNO_3/HCl)	HgS, β-HgS; HgAu

Sediment Oven-Drying Experiment

An additional experiment was conducted to examine if any changes in the concentration of THg and (or) Hg(II)$_R$ occur when previously wetted sediment is dried, as can occur naturally during summer when river waters recede to base flow or when mobilized sediment is redeposited in environments subject to seasonal wetting and drying. The four materials (wet sediment) originally used in Experiments #1, #2, and #3, Part A, (BRC-P2, 63–250 μm; and BRC-P2, HMD-CF, and SYR-P1, all <63 μm) were re-sampled in duplicate and preserved for analysis of concentrations of THg and Hg(II)$_R$, as described below. Additional sub-samples were weighed wet and then dried in an oven at 70°C for 2 days, after which they were reweighed for the determination of the percent dry weight associated with the original wet sediment. The dried samples were also sub-sampled in duplicate for analysis of the concentrations of THg and Hg(II)$_R$. The concentrations of these two Hg species, and the calculated %Hg(II)$_R$, before and after drying were then compared.

Statistical Analyses

Arithmetic means were calculated in cases where more than one analytical replicate was assayed and are represented as such in the tables and graphics. When the number of observations (n) is equal to two (n=2), analytical error is expressed as the absolute deviation from the mean ($|X_1 - X_2|/2$) or in terms of a percentage when indicated, as the relative percent deviation (RPDEV) and calculated as

$$RPDEV = |X_1 - X_2|/2/mean * 100. \tag{1}$$

When n>2, analytical error is expressed as the standard deviation or in terms of a percentage when indicated, as the relative percent standard deviation (RPSD). The single-factor analysis of variance (ANOVA) routine in Microsoft Excel 2007 (Microsoft Corp.) was used to assess significant differences in MeHg concentration among treatment pairs associated with Experiment #3, Part B (Sediment mixing/MeHg production). The allowable Type II Error probability level (P) set for this analysis was set at 5% (that is, statistically significant differences were reported if P≤0.05).

Assays

Total Mercury

Sediment collected prior to slurry preparation (Part A) and collected after centrifugation of solids at the end of the Hg(II)$_R$ time course (Part A) were preserved frozen (-80°C) for subsequent THg quantification as per a standard USGS method (Olund and others, 2004), with modifications to the sample digestion. After thawing, approximately 0.1 g of sediment (exact weight measured) was initially digested with aqua regia (2 mL of concentrated HNO$_3$ and 6 mL of concentrated HCl) in Teflon bombs overnight at room temperature. Subsequently, 22 mL of 5% BrCl was added to each sample, and the bombs were heated to 50°C in an oven overnight. Once cooled, a 5-mL sub-sample was transferred into a pre-combusted glass container. The digestate was analyzed on an Automated Mercury Analyzer (Tekran Model 2600, Tekran, Inc., Canada), according to USEPA Method 1631, Revision E (U.S. Environmental Protection Agency, 2002). This method is based on the stannous (tin) chloride (SnCl$_2$) reduction of Hg(II) to gaseous Hg(0), trapping Hg(0) on Au-plated sand, thermal desorption, and quantification of Hg(0) via cold vapor atomic fluorescence spectrometry.

Each analytical batch of samples was accompanied by the analysis of the following quality-assurance (QA) samples:

(1) One certified reference material sample,

(2) One matrix spike sample,

(3) One analytical duplicate,

(4) One method blank, and

(5) Calibration standards prepared from a NIST-certified commercial HgCl$_2$ stock.

The method detection limit at the level of the Tekran analyzer was 0.05 ng/L of aqueous digest, giving a sediment dry weight detection limit of approximately 0.5 ng/g (as run), depending on the wet sediment mass digested and its water content. The average (± standard error) recovery of the certified reference material (IAEA 405, estuarine sediment, THg certified value of 0.81 μg/g) was 99±3% (n=4). The average matrix spike recovery was 108±5% (n=4). The average RPDEV for duplicate analyses was 6.9±1.2% (n=29). The average RPSD for triplicate analyses of sequentially extracted samples was 18.9±8.7% (n=15).

Reactive Mercury

Sediment "reactive" mercury ($Hg(II)_R$) is methodologically defined as the fraction of total Hg(II), which has NOT been chemically altered (for example, digested, oxidized, or chemically preserved apart from freezing), that is readily reduced to elemental Hg(0) by an excess of $SnCl_2$ over an exposure time of 15 minutes. This operationally defined parameter was developed as a surrogate measure of the fraction of inorganic Hg(II) that is most likely available to Hg(II)-methylating bacteria responsible for MeHg production (Marvin-DiPasquale and others, 2009a). Whole sediment sub-samples (0.1–0.2 g, exact weight recorded), collected prior to slurry preparation (Part A) and after the centrifugation and recovery of solids at the end of the $Hg(II)_R$ time course (Part A), were mixed with 10 mL of 0.5% HCl (anoxic) and preserved frozen at -80°C. Subsequently, these sub-samples were thawed and assayed for $Hg(II)_R$ as previously described (Marvin-DiPasquale and Cox, 2007).

Because the $Hg(II)_R$ assay includes a 15-minute purge-and-trap step, any Hg(0) present in the sediment prior to analysis that was trapped on the Au-plated sand trap would be misinterpreted as $Hg(II)_R$. To address this concern, all pre-slurry sediment associated with Experiments #1, #2, and #3, Part A, was re-subsampled, as were the two receiving sediment materials associated with Experiment #3, Part B. These materials were then assayed again as per the $Hg(II)_R$ protocol, with the exception that no $SnCl_2$ was added to the purging flasks and flasks that had never been exposed to $SnCl_2$ were used for this assay. Thus, any Hg trapped on the Au-plated sand trap during the standard 15-minute purging step would represent Hg(0) from the sample and not from the reduction of Hg(II) to Hg(0) by $SnCl_2$. This test would not be quantitative for all the elemental Hg(0) that may have been in the sample, but only for the dissolved gaseous fraction purged from the sample during the $Hg(II)_R$ assay.

Filtered river water collected from the pre-conditioned treatment flasks (air or N_2 purged) just prior to sediment addition (Part A), slurry samples collected during the Part A time course, and supernatant samples collected after centrifuging out the solid-phase material at the end of the time course were assayed for $Hg(II)_R$ in a manner similar to that used for sediment, except that they were assayed immediately after collection and were not preserved frozen in 0.5% HCl. These samples were not assayed for elemental Hg(0), because they had been purging continuously with either air or N_2 in the slurry flasks, and the assumption is that any dissolved gaseous elemental Hg(0) that may have been in the slurry was purged from the vessel prior to slurry sub-sampling.

Each analytical batch of $Hg(II)_R$ samples was accompanied by the analysis of the following QA samples:

(1) One analytical duplicate,

(2) Four 'bubbler' blanks, and

(3) Calibration standards prepared from a NIST-certified commercial $HgCl_2$ stock.

For the Experiments #1, #2, and #3, Part A, the average RPDEV (± standard error) for all assays conducted in duplicate for Hg(II)$_R$ slurry concentration (Part A Experiments) was 7.1±1.5% (n=28), 13.5±2.6% (n=28), and 4.6±1.5% (n=29), respectively. The average RPDEV for whole sediment Hg(II)$_R$ analyses in duplicate was 6.1±1.9% (n=10).

Methylmercury

Upon thawing, sediment samples preserved frozen for MeHg analysis, as part of the MeHg production experiment (Part B), were first sub-sampled (0.6–0.7 g wet weight) into plastic centrifuge tubes. MeHg was extracted from the sediment with 2 mL of 25% KOH/methanol (25 g of KOH dissolved in 100 mL of methanol) in a 60°C oven for 4 hours (Xianchao and others, 2005). After cooling, 8 mL of DI water was added to each centrifuge tube. The contents of each tube were then homogenized via vortex and stored frozen (-80°C) until further processing. Upon thawing, samples were centrifuged at 4,000 rpm for 15 minutes. A 0.15-mL aliquot of the extractant was sub-sampled into a trace-metal clean glass I-Chem vial. The vial was nearly filled with DI water, the pH was adjusted to 4.9 using acetate buffer, and an ethylating agent (sodium tetraethyl borate) was added. The vial was then topped off with DI water, capped with a Teflon septum screwtop cap, and shaken. MeHg was converted within the vial to volatile methyl-ethyl-mercury, which was subsequently analyzed on an automated MeHg analysis system (Brooks Rand Laboratories, Seattle, WA) using cold-vapor atomic fluorescence spectrometry detection.

Each batch of analytical samples was accompanied by the analysis of the following QA samples:

(1) One certified reference material sample,

(2) One matrix spike sample,

(3) One analytical duplicate,

(4) One method blank, and

(5) Calibration standards prepared from commercial crystalline MeHgCl and compared to a separate, commercially available MeHg standard solution.

The method detection limit at the level of the MERX analyzer was approximately 0.4 pg of MeHg (absolute), giving a dry sediment detection limit of approximately 0.01 ng/g (as run), depending on the actual mass assayed and its water content. The average (± standard error) recovery of the certified reference material (IAEA 405, estuarine sediment, MeHg certified value of 5.49 ng/g) was 104±1% (n=26). The average matrix spike recovery was 102±1% (n=50). The average RPSD for replicate analyses (n=4 in all cases) was 6.9±0.7% (n=50 sample sets).

Methylmercury Production Potential

Methylmercury production potential (MPP) was quantified for the two receiving sediment materials used in Experiment #3, Part B (ENG and DMW), using a stable isotope incubation assay initiated the day following field collection. Four sub-samples of sediment (3.0±0.1 g wet weight) per site were transferred into 13-cm^3 sealed serum vials, which were crimp-sealed with a Teflon lined stopper. The vial headspace was flushed with N$_2$ gas, and the samples were stored in the refrigerator at 5°C overnight. After 3 days, the samples were allowed to pre-incubate at

22°C for 2 hours in a temperature-controlled incubator, prior to stable isotope amendment. Following pre-incubation, 0.1 mL of an isotopically enriched solution of inorganic mercury ($^{200}HgCl_2$) was injected through the septa of each vial for a final amendment concentration of 28 ng of $^{200}Hg(II)$ per g of sediment (wet weight). The samples were vortexed for 1 minute each immediately following the isotope amendment. One of the four samples per set was immediately flash frozen in a mixture of dry ice and ethanol. This sample represented the killed control. The remaining three samples in each set were returned to the 22°C incubator, where they remained for 5 hours, after which they too were flash frozen in dry ice and ethanol. The samples were stored at -80°C until further processing.

The isotopically enriched methylmercury ($Me^{200}Hg$) produced from the $^{200}Hg(II)$ during the incubation was extracted into KOH and methanol (CH_3OH) by a method modified from Xianchao and others (2005). Upon thawing, a sub-sample (0.3−0.5 g wet weight) was removed from each serum vial and transferred into a 15-mL plastic centrifuge tube. An internal standard of isotopically enriched $Me^{199}Hg$ was added (0.15 ng) to each tube, followed by 2 mL of 25% KOH in methanol. After the centrifuge tubes were tightly capped, each tube was vortexed for 1 minute and the complete batch was placed in a 60°C oven for 4 hours. After cooling to room temperature, 8 mL of DI water was added to each centrifuge tube, which was then shaken to mix and stored frozen at -80°C until further processing.

The $Me^{200}Hg$ was subsequently quantified by a modified version of the ethylation assay (Bloom, 1989), coupled with inductive coupled plasma mass spectrometry (ICP-MS) (Hintelmann and others, 1995; Hintelmann and Evans, 1997). Upon thawing, 1 mL of the KOH/CH_3OH extract was transferred to a glass bubbler containing 100 mL of anoxic DI water and 4 mL of citrate buffer. Ethylating agent (tetraethyl borate) was added (100 μL) and the mixture was shaken and allowed to react for 15 minutes prior to purging with argon gas for an additional 20 minutes. Volatile ethylated Hg species were trapped on a carbon trap (Carbotrap®) that was in-line with the bubbler gas outflow. After purging, the gas in-flow was diverted directly to the carbon traps, which were flushed and dried for an additional 7 minutes to remove any water vapor. Each carbon trap was then removed from the bubbler and placed onto a separate gas flushing rig, where the ethylated Hg species were desorbed from the carbon trap by heating, separated via gas chromatography, and then sent through the ICP-MS (Perkin-Elmer DRC II). Calibration standards were prepared with both non-enriched MeHg and isotopically enriched $Me^{199}Hg$ and were assayed in the same way as the samples. Excess $Me^{200}Hg$ (above natural abundance levels) produced during the sediment incubation was quantified on the basis of the calibration standards and the recovery of the internal standard ($Me^{199}Hg$) added during the KOH/CH_3OH extraction step. Any excess $Me^{200}Hg$ measured in the killed controls was subtracted from the samples that had been incubated for 5 hours. A pseudo first-order rate constant for $^{200}Hg(II)$-methylation (k_{meth}, units = 1/d) was then calculated from the 'kill-corrected' incubated samples as previously described for the radiotracer $^{203}Hg(II)$-methylation assay (Marvin-DiPasquale and others, 2003).

Daily MPP rates (units = ng/g dry sediment/d) were then calculated as:

$$MPP = Hg(II)_R - Hg(II)_R \bullet EXP(-k_{meth} \bullet t), \qquad (2)$$

where t=1.0 day and $Hg(II)_R$ is the independently measured *in situ* concentration of inorganic 'reactive' mercury in nanograms per gram dry weight.

Quality Assurance included:

(1) Killed controls (as described above),

(2) Analytical triplicates,

(3) The use of an internal isotope enriched standards (Me^{199}Hg, as described above), and

(4) Calibration standards prepared from commercial crystalline MeHgCl.

The RPSD for triplicate analytical determinations of k_{meth} ranged from 4% (for DMW) to 17% (for ENG).

Sediment Bulk Density, Percent Dry Weight, Porosity, and Organic Content

Sediment bulk density, dry weight, porosity, and organic content were analyzed consecutively from single sediment sub-samples, as previously detailed (Marvin-DiPasquale and others, 2008). For material collected in September 2008 and used in Experiments #1 and #2, all these assays were conducted on the pre-slurry sediment (Part A) and the receiving sediment (Part B) soon after field collection (Fleck and others, 2011). For Experiment #3, Part A, all four measurements were reassayed on the pre-slurry sediment (collected in September 2008) prior to the remobilization experiment. The Part B receiving sediment (ENG and DMW, collected in June 2009) was also assayed for these basic sediment parameters prior to initiating the sediment mixing experiment. Because of limited sample, only sediment dry weight was measured (in triplicate) on the post-slurry recovered solids from Experiments #1, #2, and #3 (Part A).

QA was achieved by assaying duplicate or triplicate samples. The post-slurry sediment dry weight was assayed in triplicate for Experiments #1 and #2, Part A, and had an average RPSD of 4.8±1.2% (n=8). All other assays were conducted in duplicate and had an average RPDEV as follows: bulk density, 0.8±0.3% (n=5); dry weight, 0.6±0.3% (n=15); porosity, 0.7±0.2% (n=5); and organic content, 1.1±0.1% (n=5).

Total Reduced Sulfur

Sediment sub-samples (approximately 1.5 g, exact weight recorded) collected for TRS analysis at the beginning of Experiment #3, immediately prior to the addition of sediment to the slurry flasks, were preserved with the addition of 0.5 mL of 10% (w/v) zinc-acetate solution and stored frozen (-80°C) in crimp-sealed serum vials under anoxic conditions. The quantification of TRS in sediment is based on a modified version of a single step heated acid/chromium distillation procedure (Fossing and Jørgensen, 1989). Upon thawing, the contents of each vial were fully transferred to a 3-neck distillation flask. After purging with N_2 gas, 20 mL of 0.6M $CrCl_3$ in 4M HCl was added to the flask, the contents of which were subsequently heated to a boil while being stirred with a magnetic bar for 1 hour. During this distillation, the resulting sulfide gas was trapped in a solution of 10 mL of 10% (w/v) zinc-acetate containing anti-foaming agent. The resulting ZnS precipitate was subsequently sub-sampled and assayed via spectrophotometric analysis (Cline, 1969). Slurry sub-samples collected on Day=0 and Day=6 of Experiment #3, Part A, were preserved and assayed in a similar fashion.

The typical detection limit for the TRS assay is approximately 1 nmol/mL at the level of the spectrophotometric analysis. For a standard zinc-acetate trap sub-sample amount of 1.0 mL and a wet sediment weight of 1.5 g, this results in a method detection limit of approximately 0.05 µg/g wet sediment. However, this detection limit can be lowered by using larger sediment weights or zinc-acetate trap sub-sampling amounts.

Quality assurance included the following:

(1) Analytical duplicates,

(2) Matrix spikes,

(3) Method blanks, and

(4) Calibration standards (ZnS).

Certified reference material for the TRS assay is not available commercially. Calibration standards (ZnS) and matrix spike solutions were prepared by precipitating a known weight reagent grade sodium sulfide (Na_2S) crystal in 10% zinc-acetate under anoxic conditions. The average matrix spike recovery was 64±8% (n=4), with three of the four values below 75%, the laboratory threshold for qualified matrix spike data. It is unclear why the matrix spike recoveries in these cases were low. As a consequence, however, the TRS data should be viewed as estimates and largely qualitative. The average RPDEV for duplicate analyses associated with Experiment #3 whole sediment and (Part A) slurry samples was 13.3±3.0% (n=5) and 20.2±4.5% (n=11), respectively.

Iron Speciation

Sediment sub-samples (collected immediately prior to the addition of sediment to the slurry flasks) and slurry sub-samples (collected on Day=0 and Day=6) for Fe-speciation analysis during Experiment #3, Part A, were preserved by freezing (-80°C) in crimp-sealed serum vials under anoxic conditions. Three Fe-fractions (acid-extractable ferrous iron ($Fe(II)_{AE}$), amorphous (poorly-crystalline) ferric iron ($Fe(III)_a$), and crystalline ferric iron ($Fe(III)_c$) were assayed as previously described (Marvin-DiPasquale and others, 2008, 2009b).

The typical detection limit for each Fe-fraction is approximately 0.02 µg/mL at the level of the spectrophotometric analysis. Assuming a 1.0 g sediment sample and a maximum 0.1 mL and 0.01 mL sub-sample of the acid-extractable ($Fe(II)_{AE}$ and $Fe(III)_a$) and dithionite-extractable ($Fe(III)_c$) fractions, respectively, the resulting method detection limits are 0.01 mg/g wet sediment and 0.10 mg/g wet sediment, respectively.

Quality assurance included the following:

(1) Analytical duplicates,

(2) Matrix spikes for $Fe(II)_{AE}$ and $Fe(III)_c$ fractions only,

(3) Method blanks, and

(4) Calibration standards ($FeSO_4$).

Certified reference material for the various Fe-species is not commercially available. Calibration standards of $FeSO_4$ were prepared in a solution of 0.25 M hydroxylamine-HCl to inhibit Fe(II) oxidation to Fe(III). Commercially produced solid-phase $FeSO_4$ (ferrous sulfate) and Fe_2O_3 (magnetite) were used as matrix spike material for the Fe(II)$_{AE}$ and Fe(III)$_c$ fractions, respectively, with matrix spike percent recovery values of 100% (n=1) for $FeSO_4$ and 111±9% (n=2) for Fe_2O_3. No commercially available Fe(III) material was found to be appropriate for use as an 'amorphous ferric iron' (that is, Fe(III)$_a$) matrix spike. The average RPDEV for duplicate assays associated with each of the three Fe fractions in sediment was 2.3±0.7% (n=5) for Fe(II)$_{AE}$, 5.6±1.3% (n=2) for Fe(III)$_a$, and 4.3±2.2% (n=5) for Fe(III)$_c$. The average RPDEV for duplicate assays associated with each of the three Fe fractions in Experiment #3, Part A, slurry samples was 18.6±5.5% (n=12) for Fe(II)$_{AE}$, 12.2±2.5% (n=11) for Fe(III)$_a$, and 2.5±0.9% (n=12) for Fe(III)$_c$.

One unanticipated result that was noted at the end of each slurry experiment (Part A) was that after the remaining slurry had been transferred to centrifuge bottles to recover the solids, the magnetic stir bars were covered with black (magnetic) precipitate, which was presumably magnetite (Fe_3O_4). Because the exact pairing of which magnet came from which slurry flask was not noted as they were being removed, a short follow-up experiment was conducted to get an estimate of how much magnetite may have been associated with each material tested in Experiment #3, Part A. Duplicate sub-samples of sediment (10 g wet weight) were again collected from the three original mason jars of material used (BRC-P2, HMD-CF, and SYR-P1) and transferred into 1-L Erlenmeyer flasks containing approximately 1 L of DI water. The flasks were again stirred with clean magnetic stir bars (the same ones used in the original experiment), although the flasks were not purged with air or N_2 gas but simply covered with Parafilm™. The new slurries were allowed to mix continuously for 48 hours, after which the slurry was decanted and the stir bars removed. Again precipitate was observed on all the magnets, which were subsequently analyzed for Fe(III)$_c$, of which Fe_3O_4 is one component. An anoxic solution of 25 mL of citrate buffer and 0.5 g of sodium dithionite was prepared and then taken up into a 10-mL syringe with a needle tip. The precipitate was washed from each magnet into a receiving beaker with a stream of the citrate/dithionite solution (10 mL per magnet) squirted from the syringe. The solution with the precipitate particles was transferred from the beakers into crimp-sealed serum vials under anoxic conditions. The serum vials were then placed on a shaker table in an incubator set for 21°C and allowed to react overnight. The citrate/dithionite dissolved the majority of the black precipitate via reduction of Fe(III)$_c$ to Fe(II). The Fe(III)$_c$ that did go into solution was quantified in each beaker via the Ferrozine spectrophotometric method. The average RPDEV for Fe(III)$_c$ recovered from each magnet associated with the three sediment types (duplicate slurry flasks for each sediment type) was 8.6±4.0% (n=3).

Results

Part A. Sediment Mobilization Simulations—Reactive Mercury Time Course

Pre- and Post-Slurry Sediment Mercury Speciation

The initial pre-slurry sediment THg concentrations associated with the two size fractions of BRC-P2 material used for Experiments #1 and #2, Part A, differed by more than 3-fold, with higher concentrations in the finer-grained material (table 3). The initial sediment pre-slurry $Hg(II)_R$ concentration, sampled after pre-incubating at room temperature for 7 days (Experiment #1) or 28 days (Experiment #2), also differed by approximately 3-fold and also was higher in the finer-grained material used in Experiment #2 (table 3). However, the percentage of THg that was $Hg(II)_R$ (that is, $\%Hg(II)_R$) in the pre-slurry sediment was similar for both Experiment #1 (10.4%) and Experiment #2 (8.3%) (table 3). For Experiment #3, Part A (table 4), where three materials were examined simultaneously (BRC-P2, HMD-CF, and SYR-P1, all <63 μm), the initial pre-slurry sediment THg concentrations varied almost 35-fold between the highest (BRC-P2) and lowest (SYR-P1). Differences in pre-slurry sediment $Hg(II)_R$ concentrations were even more pronounced between the highest (BRC-P2) and lowest (SYR-P1), varying over 500-fold. The same trend was seen for $\%Hg(II)_R$ with a 15-fold difference between BRC-P2 and SYR-P1.

A comparison of pre-slurry Hg species concentrations with post-slurry recovered solids revealed some stark differences between the two BRC-P2 size fractions and the treatments (oxic and anoxic) tested in the first two experiments (table 3). In both Experiments #1 and #2, average THg concentration in the post-slurry recovered solids was generally lower than in the initial pre-slurry sediment. This trend was also more pronounced under oxic incubation conditions compared to anoxic incubation conditions and with the coarser-grained material (Experiment #1) compared to finer-grained material (Experiment #2). In contrast, the trends in average $Hg(II)_R$ concentrations from pre-slurry to post-slurry went in opposite directions in the two experiments, increasing approximately 4-fold in both the oxic and anoxic treatments associated with Experiment #1 (BRC-P2, 63–250 μm) and decreasing by 22% (oxic treatment) and 32% (anoxic treatment) in Experiment #2 (table 3). For Experiment #1, average $\%Hg(II)_R$ values were significantly greater in post-slurry recovered solids for both oxic (77%) and anoxic (49%) treatments compared to the pre-slurry sediment (10%) based on the propagated error terms associated with each treatment. In contrast, Experiment #2 exhibited no statistically significant difference between post-slurry solids and pre-slurry sediment $\%Hg(II)_R$ concentrations, under either oxic or anoxic treatment conditions, given the propagated errors terms in each case.

A similar examination of concentrations of Hg species of pre- and post-slurry solid-phase material was conducted for Experiment #3 (table 4). Although treatments were not done in duplicate, a number of general trends were observed. Similar to the results for the fine-grained fraction of BRC-P2 in Experiment #2, the THg concentrations for both HMD-CF and BRC-P2 (<63 μm) were notably lower in the post-slurry material, compared to the pre-slurry sediment, for both oxic and anoxic incubation conditions. The SYR-P1 material did not show a clear trend in this regard, because the overlapping error terms associated with the THg concentration indicate that there was no measureable change from pre-slurry to post-slurry in that case.

Concentrations of Hg(II)$_R$ in post-slurry recovered solids in Experiment #3 were also notably lower than those for pre-slurry sediment for HMD-CF material incubated under both oxic and anoxic conditions and for both BRC-P2 and SYR-P1 material incubated under anoxic conditions (table 4). Given the propagated errors associated with %Hg(II)$_R$, the only statistically significant differences between pre-slurry and post-slurry material seen in Experiment #3 were for the HMD-CF material, where %Hg(II)$_R$ was lower in the post-slurry recovered solids for both oxic and anoxic treatment conditions (0.7 and 0.8%, respectively), compared to the pre-slurry sediment (4.3%), mirroring the trend in Hg(II)$_R$ concentration (table 4).

Table 3. Concentrations of total mercury and reactive mercury in pre-slurry and post-slurry sediment associated with the sediment mobilization simulation Experiments #1 and #2, Part A.

[The average mercury species concentration is given, along with the error shown in ( ) and the number of observations shown in [ ]. Error terms associated n=3 or more observations represent the standard deviation, while those with n=2 observations represent the absolute value of ½ of the difference between the two measurements. **Abbreviations:** THg, total mercury; Hg(II)$_R$, reactive inorganic mercury; %, percent; ng/g, nanogram per gram dry weight; μm, micrometer; BRC-P2, bedrock contact layer−Pit 2; N$_2$, dinitrogen gas; AVG, average; <, less than]

Pre- and post-slurry treatments	THg (ng/g)			Hg(II)$_R$ (ng/g)			%Hg(II)$_R$	
Experiment #1, BRC-P2, 63–250 μm								
Pre-slurry	3,012	(198)	[4]	313	(46)	[3]	10.4	(1.7)
Post, Air-A	1,689	(50)	[2]	1054		[1]	62.4	
Post, Air-B	1,756	(97)	[2]	1619		[1]	92.2	
AVG Post-Air	1,722	(54)		1,337	(282)		77.3	(16.5)
Post, N$_2$-A	2,359	(25)	[2]	1377		[1]	58.4	
Post, N$_2$-B	2,664	(478)	[2]	1030		[1]	38.7	
AVG Post-N$_2$	2,511	(239)		1,203	(174)		48.5	(8.4)
Experiment #2, BRC-P2, <63 μm								
Pre-slurry	10,824	(382)	[3]	896	(86)	[3]	8.3	(0.8)
Post, Air-A	9,067	(1079)	[2]	763	(203)	[2]	8.4	
Post, Air-B	6,974	(723)	[2]	638	(48)	[2]	9.1	
AVG Post-Air	8,020	(649)		701	(104)		8.8	(1.5)
Post, N$_2$-A	10,997	(3290)	[2]	564	(275)	[2]	5.1	
Post, N$_2$-B	8,312	(516)	[2]	657	(104)	[2]	7.9	
AVG Post-N$_2$	9,655	(1665)		610	(147)		6.5	(1.9)

Table 4. Concentrations of total mercury and reactive mercury in pre-slurry and post-slurry sediment associated with the sediment mobilization simulation Experiment #3, Part A.

[The average mercury species concentration is given, along with the error shown in ( ) and the number of observations shown in [ ]. Error terms associated n=3 or more observations represent the standard deviation, while those with n=2 observations represent ½ of the difference between with the two measurements. **Abbreviations:** THg, total mercury; Hg(II)$_R$, reactive inorganic mercury; SYR-P1, South Yuba River–Pit 1; HMD-CF, hydraulic mining debris from eroding cliff exposure; BRC-P2, bedrock contact layer–Pit 2; %, percent; ng/g, nanogram per gram dry weight; <, less than; N$_2$, dinitrogen gas]

Pre- and post-slurry treatments	THg (ng/g)			Hg(II)$_R$ (ng/g)			%Hg(II)$_R$	
SYR-P1, <63 µm								
Pre-slurry	263	(21)	[2]	4.6	(2.2)	[3]	1.7	(0.8)
Post, air	313	(52)	[2]	4.6	(0.6)	[3]	1.5	(0.3)
Post, N$_2$	222	(29)	[2]	1.9	(0.1)	[3]	0.9	(0.1)
HMD-CF, <63 µm								
Pre-slurry	1398	(25)	[2]	60.2	(21.2)	[3]	4.3	(1.5)
Post, air	1185	(59)	[2]	8.4	(1.2)	[3]	0.7	(0.1)
Post, N$_2$	1081	(2)	[2]	8.9	(1.0)	[3]	0.8	(0.1)
BRC-P2, <63 µm								
Pre-slurry	9170	(214)	[2]	2530	(130)	[3]	27.6	(1.6)
Post, air	7634	(556)	[2]	2383	(686)	[3]	31.2	(9.3)
Post, N$_2$	7931	(967)	[2]	1831	(112)	[3]	23.1	(3.1)

Slurry Time-Course Data

Concentrations of THg and Hg(II)$_R$ in the filtered river water, sampled from the flasks immediately prior to the addition of sediment, were very low (1.8±0.2 ng/L (n=15) and <0.5 ng/L (n=14), respectively, across all three experiments), compared to the slurry concentrations after the sediment was added (figs. 4 and 5). The initial average THg concentrations associated with each Part A experiment were calculated on the basis of pre-slurry sediment THg concentrations, the mass of sediment added to each flask, and the known volume of filtered river water at the beginning of each experiment. The initial average THg concentrations in each slurry treatment flask were:

(1) Experiment #1 (BRC-P2, 63–250 µm), 12,050±400 ng/L;

(2) Experiment #2 (BRC-P2, <63 µm), 32,440±1,990 ng/L;

(3) Experiment #3 (SYR-P1, <63 µm), 1,810±10 ng/L;

(4) Experiment #3 (HMD-CF, <63 µm), 10,130±130 ng/L; and

(5) Experiment #3 (BRC-P2, <63 µm), 52,420±80 ng/L.

The Hg(II)$_R$ concentration in the suspended slurry flasks over time for Experiments #1 and #2 is depicted in figure 4. The same type of data for Experiment #3 is depicted in figure 5. In all five time-course experiments, Hg(II)$_R$ concentrations were either greater than or essentially the same under the oxic treatment compared to the anoxic treatment. However, the temporal trends and the magnitude of difference between oxic and anoxic treatments varied for each sediment type tested.

Concentrations of THg in the supernatant, derived from centrifuging the remaining slurry at the end of the mobilization simulation experiments, were surprisingly high. The supernatant THg concentrations in Experiments #1 and #2 could not be accurately quantified, because the amount of THg in the sample exceeded the analytical working range and the entire sample volumes were used for the analyses, precluding reruns. However, for Experiment #3, small sub-samples of the supernatant were assayed and THg concentrations were successfully quantified, and ranged from 3,110 to 18,560 ng/L for the two BRC-P2 flasks, 928 to 1,070 ng/L for the two HMD-CF flasks, and 234 to 243 ng/L for the two SYR-P1 flasks. Physical observation of the centrifuge containers immediately after centrifugations revealed a slightly cloudy and (or) colored aqueous phase, indicative of very fine clay-size particles that remained in the supernatant, even after repeated and prolonged centrifugation. The elevated THg concentrations measured in the supernatant are attributed to Hg associated with these very fine suspended particles. Calculations that are based on centrifugation speed, time, and radius suggest that the particles remaining in the supernatant ranged in size from approximately less than 0.3 μm (assuming spherical particles only) to less than 3 μm (assuming non-spherical particle shapes), thus covering the range from coarse clay (2–0.2 μm) to fine clay (<0.2 μm). On the basis of the volume of slurry remaining at the end of the experiment, the quantity of THg lost to the supernatant fraction during centrifugation was 2.5–15.0 μg THg (BRC-P2), 0.76–0.86 μg THg (HMD-CF), and 0.18 μg THg (SYR-P1). Overall, these losses accounted for 81±29% of the observed decrease in THg concentration between pre-slurry sediment and post-slurry recovered solids across all treatments in Experiment #3.

For Experiment #3, Part A, the MeHg concentration in HMD-CF post-slurry solids was 2-fold (oxic treatment) to 3-fold (anoxic treatment) greater than the pre-slurry sediment, suggesting that there was MeHg production in the HMD-CF slurry flasks during the incubation (fig. 6). A similar trend was not seen for either the BRC-P2 or the SYR-P1 material. Concentrations of MeHg were not measured in Experiments #1 or #2, Part A, so it is not known whether or not a similar effect would have been observed.

Total Reduced Sulfur and Iron-Speciation Data

The three types of material tested in Experiment #3, Part A, differed greatly in terms of their pre-slurry TRS and Fe-species concentrations (table 5). The TRS concentration of the BRC-P2 material (0.357±0.032) was more than 4-fold and 70-fold greater than the concentrations associated with the SYR-P1 (0.081±0.017) and HMD-CF materials (0.005±0.001), respectively. Total iron (Fe$_T$) in pre-slurry sediment was dominated by Fe(III)$_c$ for both BRC-P2 and HMD-CF materials (≥97% of Fe$_T$). A small fraction of poorly crystalline Fe(III)$_a$ was observed in the BRC-P2 (3% of Fe$_T$) and HMD-CF (0.5% of Fe$_T$) materials, and Fe(II)$_{AE}$ was less than 0.3% of Fe$_T$ in both cases. For SYR-P1, Fe(III)$_c$, Fe(II)$_{AE}$, and Fe(III)$_a$ comprised 64, 36 and <0.3% of the Fe$_T$, respectively.

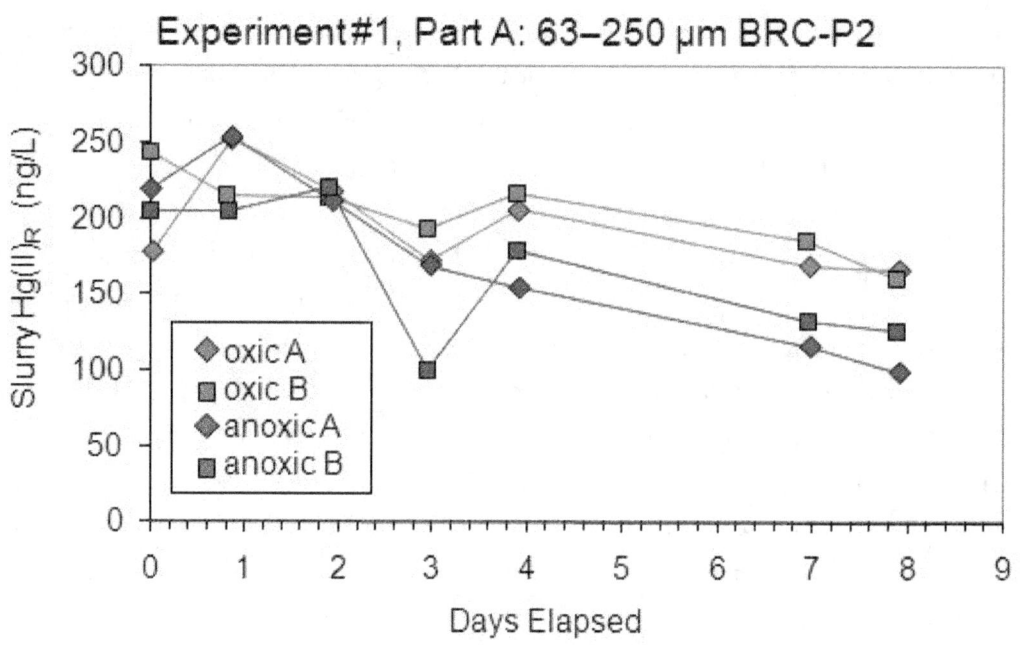

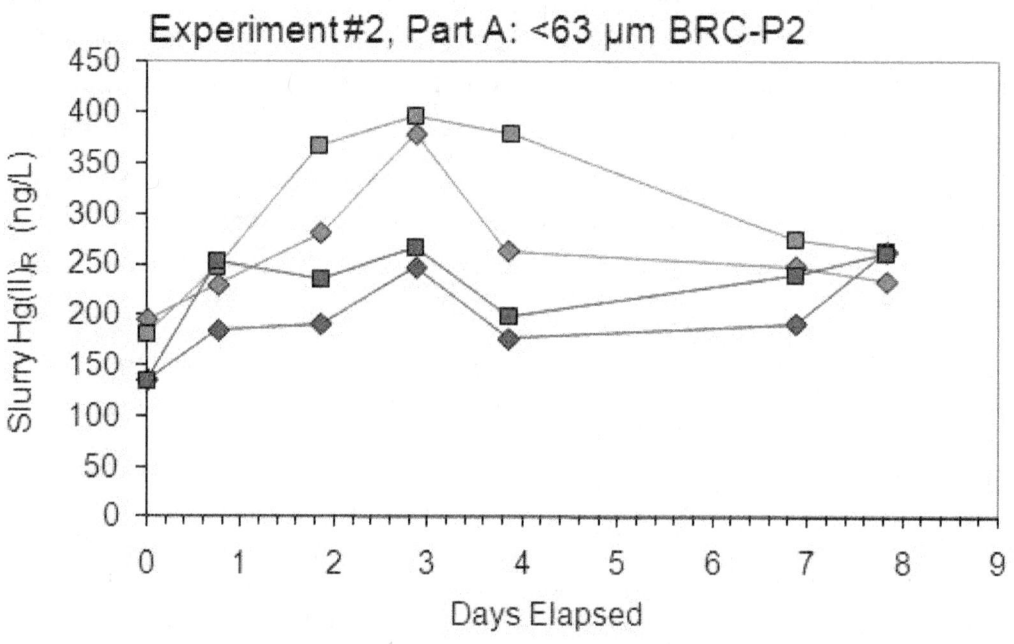

Figure 4. Time course of slurry reactive mercury (Hg(II)$_R$) concentration associated with Experiments #1 and #2, Part A. The sediment used in Experiment #1 and Experiment #2 was the 63–250 μm Bedrock contact layer – Pit 2 (BRC-P2) and the <63 μm BRC-P2, respectively.

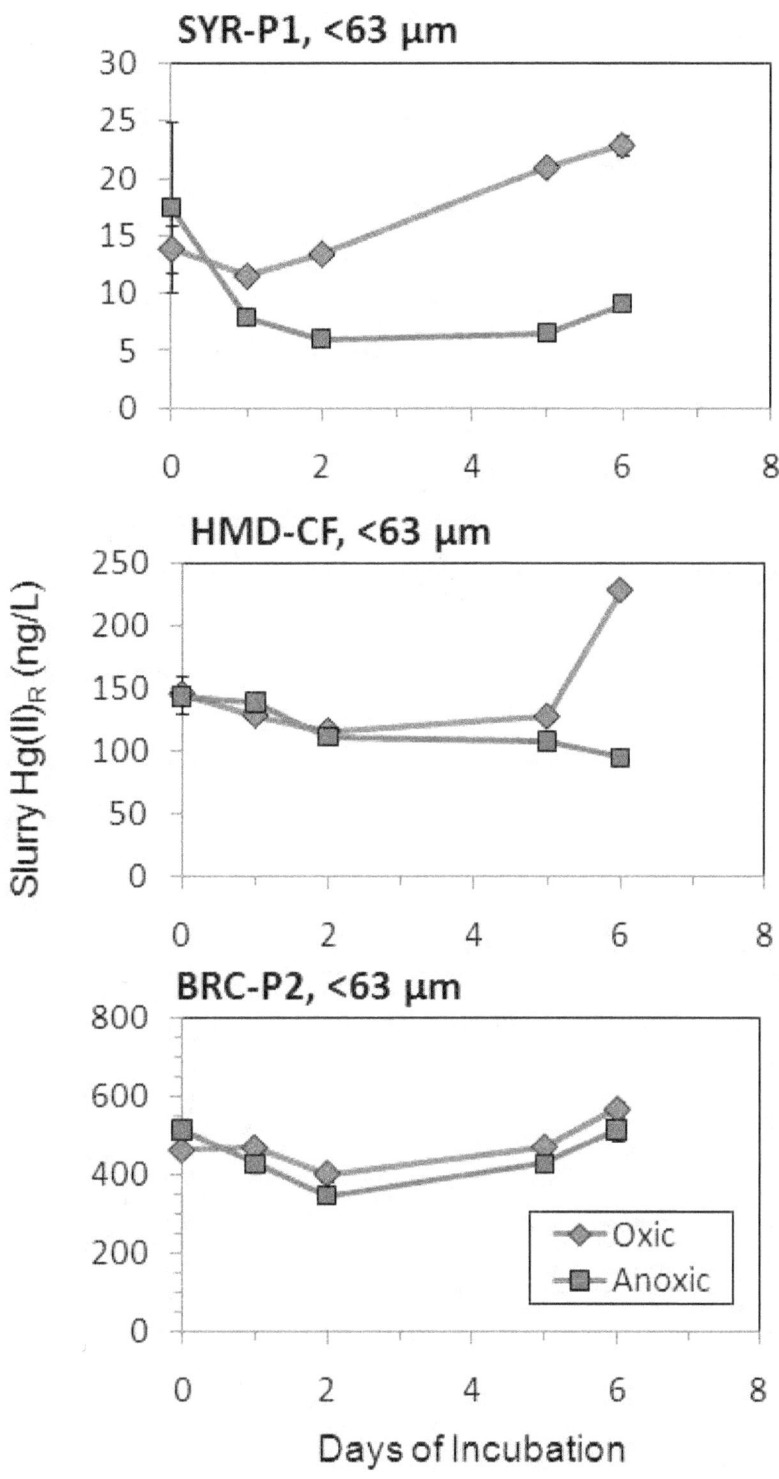

Figure 5. Time course of slurry reactive mercury (Hg(II)$_R$) concentration associated with Experiment #3, Part A. The sediment used was from the <63 µm size fraction and included South Yuba River – Pit 1 (SYR-P1), hydraulic mining debris – cliff face (HMD-CF), and Bedrock contact layer – Pit 2 (BRC-P2).

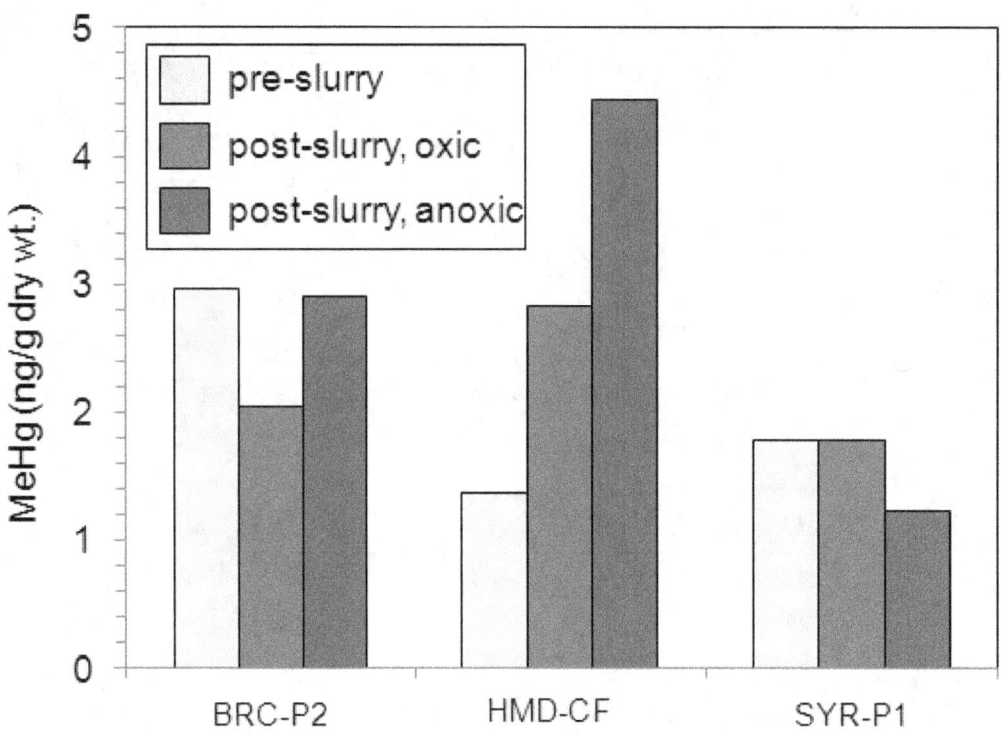

Figure 6. Bar graph of methylmercury (MeHg) concentration in pre-slurry sediment and post-slurry recovered solids, incubated under oxic or anoxic slurry conditions, associated with Experiment #3, Part A. The sediment used was from the <63 μm size fraction and included and Bedrock contact layer – Pit 2 (BRC-P2), hydraulic mining debris – cliff face (HMD-CF), and South Yuba River – Pit 1 (SYR-P1).

Once the sediment was mixed with the pre-conditioned filtered river water, changes were seen in slurry concentrations of both TRS and Fe species from the beginning to the end of the mobilization simulation. In five of the six flasks, TRS concentrations at the end of the slurry experiment (Day=6) were greater than the concentration at the beginning of the experiment (Day=0); the exception was the HMD-CF material incubated under anoxic conditions (fig. 7).

A comparison of the measured Fe-species concentrations at the beginning (Day=0) and end (Day=6) of Experiment #3, Part A, also indicated some changes between Fe-pools during the week-long mobilization simulation (fig. 8). The strongest trend was seen with the SYR-P1 material, with both Fe(II)$_{AE}$ (fig. 8A) and Fe(III)$_a$ (fig. 8B) decreasing from the beginning to the end of the experiment under both oxic and anoxic treatments. Crystalline Fe(III)$_c$ was well conserved from the beginning to the end of the experiment for BRC-P2 and HMD-CF material and showed an increase over time in the case of the SYR-P1 material incubated anoxically (fig. 8C).

Table 5. Characterization of non-mercury parameters associated with pre-slurry sediment used in Experiment #3, Part A.

[The associated error with each value is shown in ( ) and is based on n=2 replicates and represents ½ of the difference between the two measurements. When no error term is given, n=1. **Abbreviations:** BRC-P2, bedrock contact layer–Pit 2; HMD-CF, hydraulic mining debris from the eroding cliff face; SYR-P1, South Yuba River–Pit 1; <63 µm, less than 63 micrometer size fraction; LOI, organic content via weight loss on ignition; TRS, total reduced sulfur; $Fe(II)_{AE}$, acid extractable ferrous iron; $Fe(III)_a$, amorphous ferric iron; $Fe(III)_c$, crystalline ferric iron; Fe_T, total iron measured ($Fe(II)_{AE} + Fe(III)_a + Fe(III)_c$); %, percent; mg/g dry wt, milligram per gram dry weight; g/cm^3, gram per cubic centimeter]

Parameter	Units	BRC-P2, <63 µm		HMD-CF, <63 µm		SYR-P1, <63 µm	
LOI	%	4.3	(0.1)	5.9	(0.1)	6.5	(0.1)
TRS	mg/g dry wt	0.357	(0.032)	0.005	(0.001)	0.081	(0.017)
$Fe(II)_{AE}$	mg/g dry wt	0.07	(0.00)	0.14	(0.00)	6.57	(0.12)
$Fe(III)_a$	mg/g dry wt	0.87	(0.04)	0.25	(0.02)	<0.05	
$Fe(III)_c$	mg/g dry wt	30.39	(0.26)	48.14	(0.41)	11.9	(0.91)
magnetic-Fe [1]	mg/g dry wt	0.58		0.91		2.08	
Fe_T	mg/g dry wt	31.33	(0.27)	48.53	(0.41)	18.5	(0.92)
$Fe(II)_{AE}$	% of Fe_T	0.2		0.3		35.5	
$Fe(III)_a$	% of Fe_T	2.8		0.5		0.3	
$Fe(III)_c$	% of Fe_T	97.0		99.2		64.2	
magnetic-Fe [a]	% of Fe_T	1.9		1.9		11.2	
Dry weight	%	49.9	(0.0)	62.1	(0.0)	59.2	(0.1)
Bulk density	g/cm^3	1.39	(0.00)	1.19	(0.02)	0.91	(0.01)

[1] Magnetic-Fe is a subset of the $Fe(III)_c$ fraction, and likely largely magnetite (Fe_3O_4). The concentrations reported are considered to be estimates, because they were derived from a separate experimental assessment carried out after the initial slurry Experiment #3 was conducted (see text).

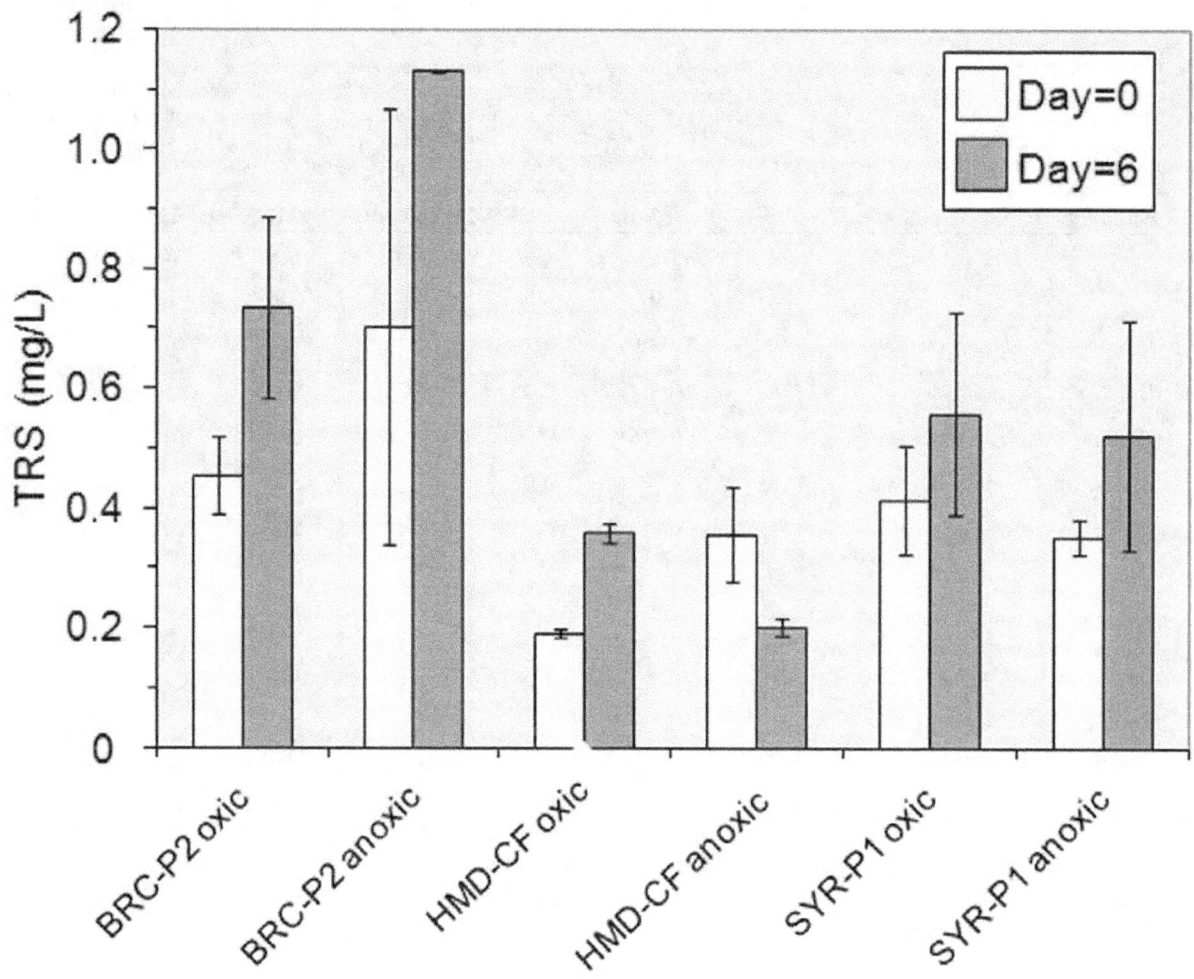

Figure 7. Bar graph of total reduced sulfur (TRS) concentration in the six slurry flasks at the beginning (Day=0) and end (Day=6) of Experiment #3, Part A. The sediment used was from the <63 μm size fraction and included and Bedrock contact layer–Pit 2 (BRC-P2), hydraulic mining debris–cliff face (HMD-CF), and South Yuba River–Pit 1 (SYR-P1). Error bars represent the maximum and minimum values for n=2 measurements.

Because of visible loss of magnetic minerals (presumably magnetite and (or) maghemite) on the stir bars during Experiment #3, additional experiments were done to quantify this effect. The quantifiable $Fe(III)_c$ associated with the stir bars (magnetic-Fe) ranged from 0.58 mg/g dry weight (BRC-P2) to 2.08 mg/g dry weight (SYR-P1) and accounted for 1.9, 1.9, and 11.2% of Fe_T for Experiment #3 (Part A) in BRC-P2, HMD-CF, and SYR-P1 material, respectively (table 5).

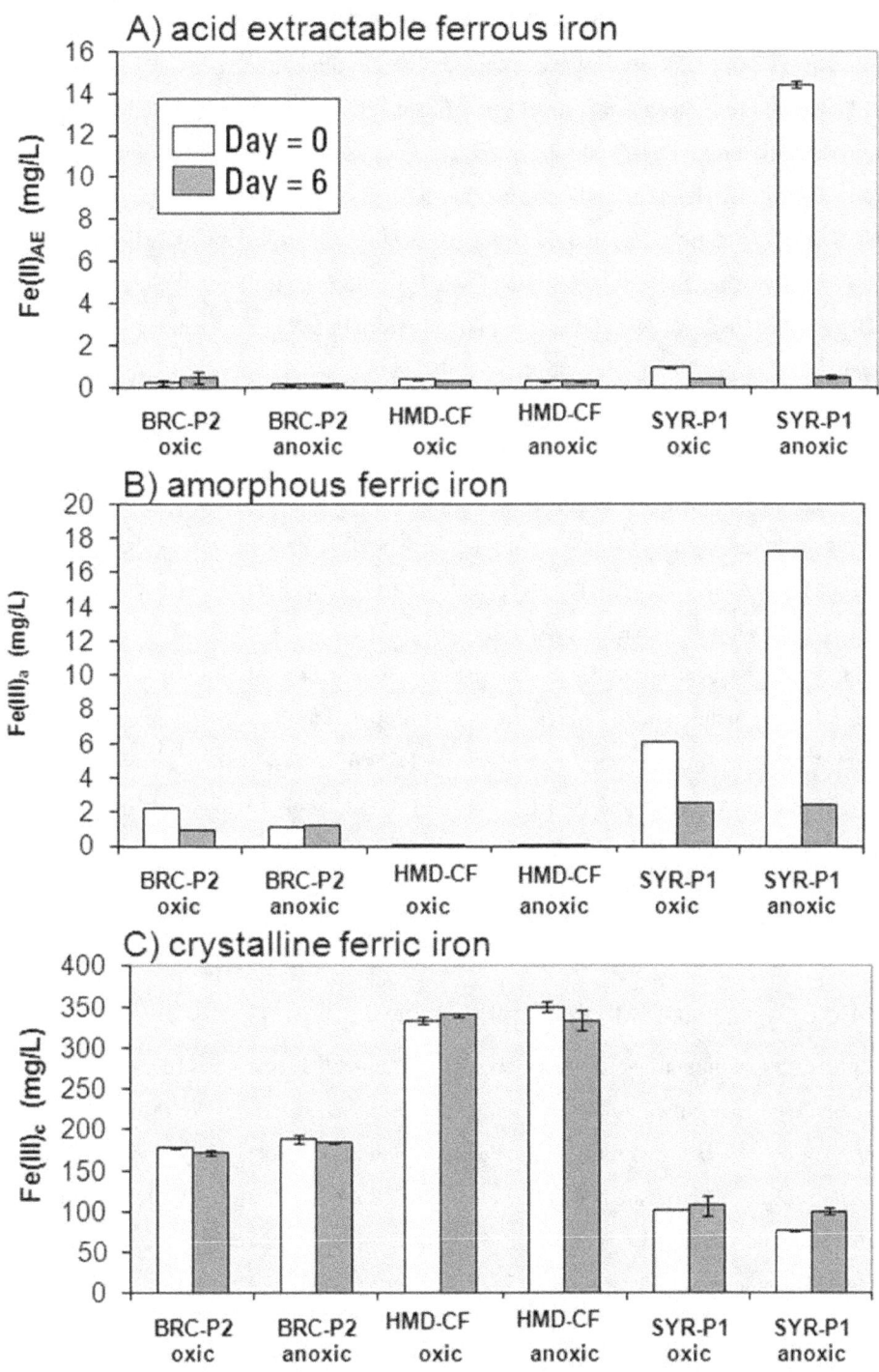

Figure 8. Bar graphs of *A)* acid extractable ferrous iron (Fe(II)$_{AE}$), *B)* amorphous ferric iron (Fe(III)$_a$), and *C)* crystalline ferric iron (Fe(III)$_c$) in the six slurry flasks at the beginning (Day=0) and end (Day=6) of Experiment #3, Part A. The sediment used was from the <63 µm size fraction and included and Bedrock contact layer–Pit 2 (BRC-P2), hydraulic mining debris–cliff face (HMD-CF), and South Yuba River–Pit 1 (SYR-P1). Error bars represent the maximum and minimum values for n=2 measurements.

Part B. Sediment Mixing / Methylmercury Production Experiments

When spiking sediment BRC-P2 (63–250 μm) was added to receiving sediment SYR-MC (<1,000 μm) in sediment mixing Experiment #1, Part B, there was no statistically significant MeHg formation over time in either the non-amended control or the amended mixture (fig. 9A). Similarly, results from sediment mixing Experiments #2, Part B, resulted in no statistically significant MeHg formation when the spiking sediment was BRC-P2 (<63 μm) and the receiving sediment was SYR-P1 (<63 μm) (fig. 9B). In contrast, results from Experiment #3 showed statistically significant MeHg production when the spiking sediment was BRC-P2 (<63 μm) and the receiving sediment was either from ENG or DMW (fig. 10). The HMD-CF spiking material used in Experiment #3 also resulted in statistically significant increases in MeHg concentration by the end of the incubation period, compared to the control, when the receiving sediment was either ENG or DMW, although these increases were not as large as those seen when BRC-P2 was used for the spiking material (fig. 10). There were no statistically significant differences in MeHg concentration at the end of the experiment (relative to the control) when SYR-P1 was the spiking material, for any receiving sediment or pre-treatment combination. The difference in $Hg(II)_R$ from the pre-treatment of the 'spiking' materials (either oxic or anoxic pre-treatment in Part A) appeared not to result in statistically significant differences in the amount of MeHg production in Part B.

In addition to comparing MeHg concentrations on Day=6 in spike-amended samples to non-spiked controls, MeHg concentrations on Day=0 in amended mixtures were also compared to the non-spiked control treatments. Results for these Day=0 comparisons were similar to those for Day=6, with statistically greater MeHg concentrations (relative to non-spiked controls) observed for BRC-P2 and HMD-CF spiking materials in combination with both ENG and DMW receiving sediment (fig. 10).

Additional Sediment Characterization

Assessment of Elemental Hg(0) Associated with the $Hg(II)_R$ Assay

Tests conducted with pre-slurry sediment from Experiments #1, #2, and #3, Part A, as well as with both receiving sediment types associated with Experiment #3, Part B, indicate that very little (if any) of the $Hg(II)_R$ measured was actually elemental Hg(0) associated with the sample prior to reducing Hg(II) to Hg(0) with $SnCl_2$. The greatest amount of Hg(0) trapped in the absence of $SnCl_2$ was associated with the 63–250 μm BRC-P2 material (Experiment #1, Part A), which accounted for only 1.5% of the original $Hg(II)_R$ measurement. For the <63 μm BRC-P2 material (Experiment #2, Part A), elemental Hg(0) accounted for <0.02% of the original $Hg(II)_R$ measurement. For Experiment #3, Part A, elemental Hg(0) accounted for <0.03 and <0.07% of the original $Hg(II)_R$ measured in the BRC-P2 and HMD-CF material, respectively, and was undetectable in the SYR-P1 material. Elemental Hg(0) was also undetectable in the ENG and DMW material associated with Experiment #3, Part B.

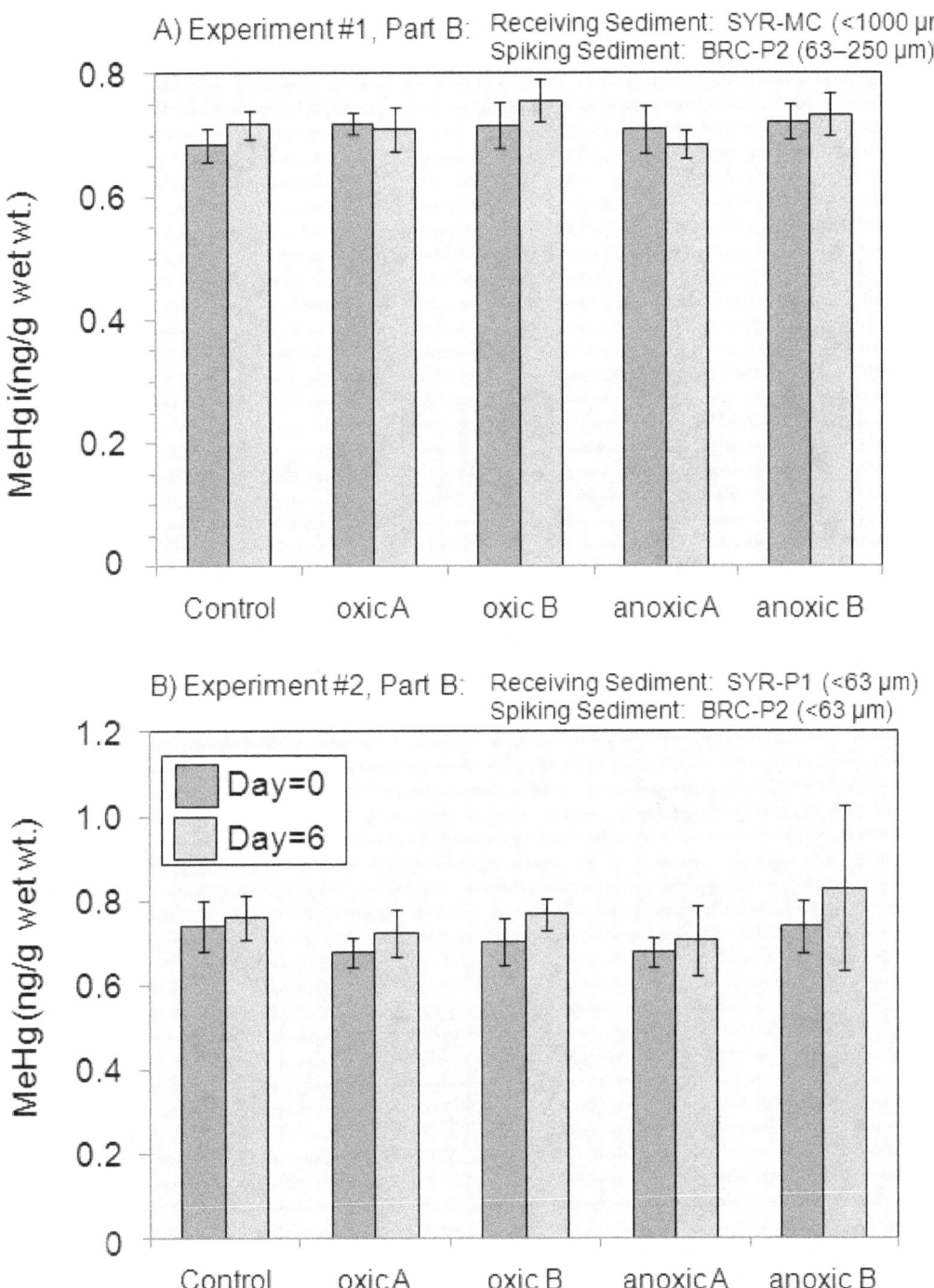

Figure 9. Bar graphs showing sediment methylmercury (MeHg) concentration at the beginning (Day=0) and end (Day=6) of the incubation period for all treatments associated with the sediment mixing Experiments #1 (A) and #2 (B), Part B. The receiving sediment used in each case was <1000 µm South Yuba Bar graphs showing sediment methylmercury (MeHg) concentration at the beginning (Day=0) and end (Day=6) of the incubation period for all treatments associated with the sediment mixing Experiments #1 (A) and #2 (B), Part B. The receiving sediment used in each case was <1000 µm South Yuba River–main channel (SYR-MC) and <63 µm South Yuba River–Pit 1 (SYR-P1), respectively. The spiking sediment used in each case was 63–250 µm Bedrock contact–Pit 2 (BRC-P2) and <63 µm BRC-P2, respectively. Error bars represent the standard deviation from the mean for n=4 measurements..

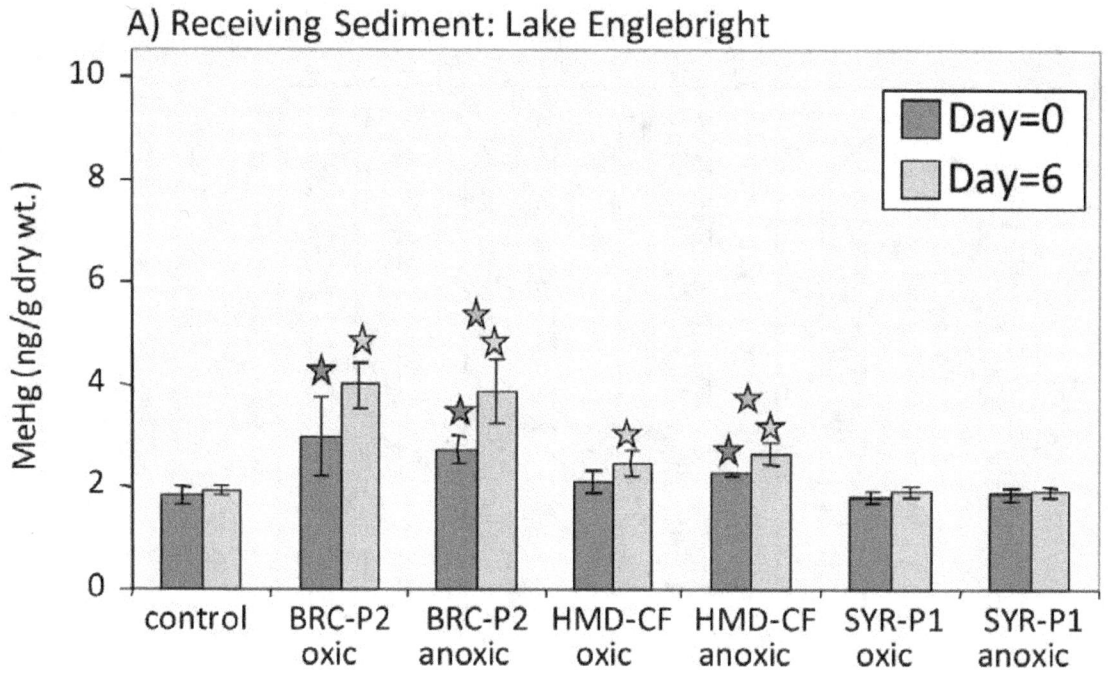

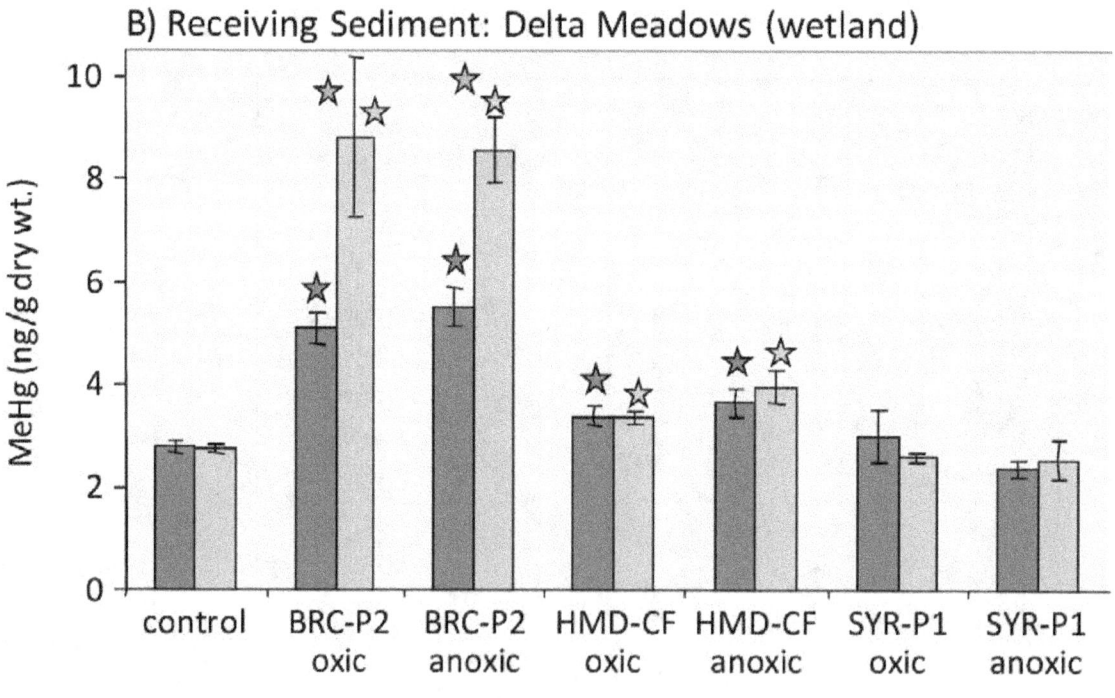

Figure 10. Bar graphs showing methylmercury (MeHg) concentration at the beginning (Day=0) and end (Day=6) of the incubation period for all treatments associated with sediment mixing Experiment #3, Part B, where the receiving sediment was from A) Englebright Lake and B) Delta Meadows wetland. Error bars represent ±1 standard deviation (n=4). Significant differences (P < 0.05) are indicated by the following: Day 0 treatment vs Day 0 control (★), Day 6 treatment vs Day 6 control (☆), Day 0 vs Day 6 for a single grouping (★). Error bars represent the standard deviation from the mean for n=4 measurements.

Assessment of Hg(0) associated with the Hg(II)$_R$ assay was also made for samples used in the oven-drying experiment. Material was tested both pre- and post-oven drying. In these assays, elemental Hg(0) accounted for 0.2–3.7% of the Hg measured as Hg(II)$_R$, with an average (± standard error) of 1.7±0.4% (n=8) across all samples and treatments. As with the Experiment #3 materials, the highest observed percentage was associated with the BRC-P2 63–250 μm size fraction (pre-oven treatment). It should be emphasized that these assessments were not quantitative for all the Hg(0) that may have existed in these samples, but only for the fraction that may have been trapped during the Hg(II)$_R$ assay.

Oven-Drying Experiment

There was no appreciable change in the THg concentration pre- versus post-oven drying of sediment at 70°C for 48 hrs (fig. 11A). However, there was a marked increase in both Hg(II)$_R$ concentration and %Hg(II)$_R$ in the case of the SYR-P1 <63 μm and the BRC-P2 63–250 μm materials, with the most pronounced increases associated with the latter sediment (figs. 11B and 11C).

Experiment #3, Part C: Sequential Extraction of Pre-Slurry Sediment

The sequential extraction scheme applied to the three pre-slurry sediment samples used in Experiment #3, Part A (BRC-P2, HMD-CF, and SYR-P1; all <63μm), provides critical information on the forms of Hg that likely exist in these materials, their concentrations, and their relative proportions (tables 2 and 6). Results from this characterization indicate that there is very little easily extracted Hg (≤0.1% of THg), represented by fractions F1 (water-soluble Hg salts) and F2 (weak acid [pH=2] soluble/extractable Hg, for example, HgO), in any of the three materials examined (table 6). The vast majority of all the Hg existed in the F3, F4, and F5 fractions. The F3 (1N KOH extractable) fraction represents both organic Hg (for example, MeHg) and inorganic Hg(II) sorbed onto the surface of particles (likely associated with organic coatings on particles) and comprised 36.8, 55.2, and 3.8% of the SYR-P1, HMD-CF, and BRC-P2 materials, respectively. The F4 fraction (12N HNO$_3$ extractable) is the sole fraction in which elemental Hg(0) is quantitatively associated, as well as some calomel (Hg$_2$Cl$_2$) and perhaps some Hg-Au amalgam. The F4 fraction comprised 56.9, 41.4, and 72.2% of the SYR-P1, HMD-CF, and BRC-P2 material, respectively. The F5 (aqua regia extractable) fraction is the fraction in which most Hg-Au amalgam and the two forms of cinnabar (HgS and β-HgS) are quantitatively associated (table 2). The F5 fraction comprised 6.1, 3.4, and 23.9% of the SYR-P1, HMD-CF, and BRC-P2 material, respectively.

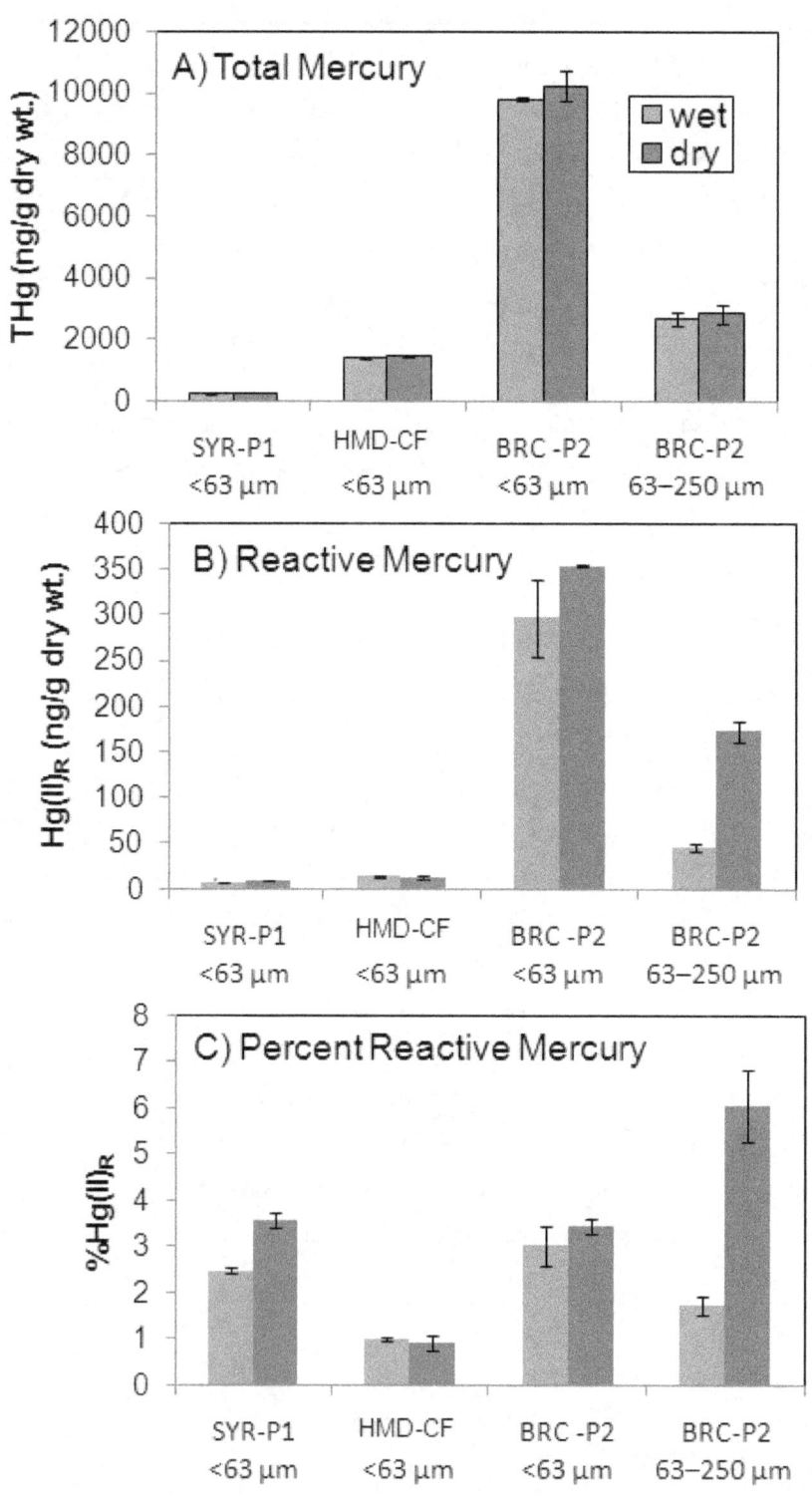

Figure 11. Bar graphs showing the pre-oven (wet) versus post-over (dry) sediment concentrations of A) total mercury (THg), B) reactive mercury (Hg(II)$_R$), and C) percent reactive mercury (%Hg(II)$_R$) for materials used in Part A (sediment mobilization simulation) experiments. Error bars represent the maximum and minimum values for n=2 measurements.

Table 6. Experiment #3, Part C—Sequential extraction analysis results for pre-slurry spiking materials.

[The standard error associated with each value is given in ( ) and is based on n=3 replicates. All materials assayed were <63 μm size fraction. See table 2 for the dominant Hg species associated with each SE fraction. **Abbreviations:** SE, sequential extraction; Hg, mercury; %THg, percent of total mercury; ng/g dry wt, nanogram per gram dry weight; SYR-P1, South Yuba River−Pit 1; HMD-CF, hydraulic mining debris from the eroding cliff face; BRC-P2, bedrock contact−Pit 2]

Sediment	SE fraction	Hg (ng/g dry wt)		%THg	
SYR-P1	F1	0.31	(0.01)	0.12	(0.00)
	F2	0.23	(0.01)	0.09	(0.00)
	F3	96.2	(3.1)	36.8	(1.4)
	F4	149	(4)	56.9	(2.0)
	F5	15.8	(0.8)	6.0	(0.3)
	TOTAL	**261**	**(5)**	**100.0**	**(2.5)**
HMD-CF	F1	0.13	(0.03)	0.01	(0.00)
	F2	0.63	(0.04)	0.05	(0.00)
	F3	713	(69)	55.2	(6.6)
	F4	534	(3)	41.4	(2.9)
	F5	43.6	(58.7)	3.4	(4.6)
	TOTAL	**1,291**	**(91)**	**100.0**	**(8.5)**
BRC-P2	F1	0.80	(0.10)	0.01	(0.00)
	F2	3.3	(0.2)	0.03	(0.00)
	F3	396	(124)	3.8	(1.3)
	F4	7,485	(638)	72.2	(9.8)
	F5	2,481	(880)	23.9	(8.9)
	TOTAL	**10,366**	**(1,094)**	**100.0**	**(13.3)**

Discussion

The laboratory experiments described in this report, conducted as part of a larger assessment of Hg-contaminated sediment in the SYR-HC confluence area, were designed to answer two overarching questions:

(1) *Does the remobilization of previously buried, Hg-contaminated sediment from historical mining affect the speciation (chemical composition) of Hg associated with the sediment?*

(2) *Does the inorganic Hg(II) associated with remobilized sediment enhance the production of MeHg in downstream habitats once the Hg-enriched particulates are redeposited?*

The results from the laboratory experiments described herein clearly indicate that the answer to these two questions is '*yes.*' However, the degree of the observed response in both cases was strongly dependent on the physical and chemical nature of mobilized material as well as that of the sediment onto which the mobilized material is ultimately deposited and mixed.

A third question associated with the larger project is:

(3) *Can contemporary suction-dredging technology be used as a viable approach to remove Hg, in the form of elemental Hg(0) and Hg-Au amalgam, from historically contaminated areas?*

Although the consequences of dredging a Hg-hotspot were not directly tested as part of the field or laboratory components of the study, the results of the laboratory experiments do provide some insight into this question as it pertains to the fate and transport of fine Hg-rich particles and is taken up in the last part of the discussion section.

Sediment Mobilization in Surface Water

The original idea behind the Part A slurry experiments (sediment mobilization simulations) was to directly measure changes in $Hg(II)_R$ when sediment that is initially in chemically reducing conditions becomes resuspended and transported in oxygenated water, such as the scenario of anoxic buried sediments being eroded and transported in a typical flowing river. The laboratory conditions that were chosen were intended to simulate what takes place when sediment is mobilized by either natural forces (such as bank erosion or streambed remobilization during high-flow conditions) or human manipulation (such as suction dredging), because surface water in river systems is almost always well oxygenated. Thus, the anoxic treatments (N_2-purged flasks) served as a 'control' to examine the direct influence of dissolved O_2 (in the oxic treatments) on $Hg(II)_R$ concentration in the mobilization simulations. The decision to purge, continuously stir, and sub-sample the slurry over multiple days was based on the idea that, once mobilized, fine particles (for example, in the silt-clay size range, <63 µm, and especially in the clay size range, <2 µm) do not readily settle out of the water column, even after days, as was clearly demonstrated in the tank experiment conducted as part of the field study portion of this project (Fleck and others, 2011). For similar reasons, the focus of the 'mobilization simulation' experiments was on the smallest size fraction (<63 µm) of the material collected in the field, except in the case of Experiment #1 where the BRC-P2 63–250 µm size fraction was examined (table 1).

The hypothesized increase in Hg(II)$_R$ concentration under oxic conditions was based on the results from a similar experiment previously conducted with deeply buried sediment (150–175 cm below the sediment-water interface) collected from Alviso Slough in South SFB (Marvin-DiPasquale and Cox, 2007). In that study, Hg(II)$_R$ concentrations in the oxic slurry increased 40- to 60-fold (relative to starting concentrations) over the week-long slurry experiment. The hypothesis was further based on field data from two recent studies, one including eight diverse river systems (Marvin-DiPasquale and others, 2009a) and the other from a suite of wetland sites in the Sacramento River watershed (Marvin-DiPasquale and others, 2009b). Both studies involved a suite of sediment samples covering a range of natural geochemical gradients and showed that the %Hg(II)$_R$ increases as sediment conditions become less chemically reducing and (or) sediment contains decreasing concentrations of TRS. This body of research, as well as other unpublished data by the same research group, points to the idea that Hg(II) that is strongly bound to reduced sulfur minerals is not readily 'reactive' (not measurable as Hg(II)$_R$). Thus, when mobilized sediment particles containing TRS minerals (for example, FeS, FeS$_2$, and other sulfides that may include Hg) become oxidized, TRS concentrations decrease, and an increasing proportion of the associated Hg(II) is measured as Hg(II)$_R$. In essence, it is the particles with which the Hg(II) is associated that are being chemically altered (oxidized), not the Hg itself. However, this chemical alteration of the particulate mineral phase directly affects Hg(II) binding and availability, at least insofar as the methodologically defined Hg(II)$_R$ assay.

The results from the current suite of experiments are consistent with the above hypothesized scenario in two important aspects. First, oxic slurry Hg(II)$_R$ concentrations were always greater than or similar to anoxic slurry Hg(II)$_R$ concentrations in all three experiments and in all four materials tested (figs. 4 and 5). Second, at the end of each slurry experiment, the %Hg(II)$_R$ was higher in the recovered solid-phase material associated with the oxic treatment, as compared to the anoxic treatment, with the exception of Experiment #3 HMD-CF material in which there was no notable difference in %Hg(II)$_R$ between oxic and anoxic treatments (tables 3 and 4).

The magnitude of the Hg(II)$_R$ increase under oxic conditions was generally much less dramatic in the current study (figs. 4 and 5), compared with that seen in the Alviso Slough study (see fig. 13 in Marvin-Dipasquale and Cox, 2007). One explanation for this stems from the fact that, as an estuarine sediment, the Alviso Slough substrate contained much greater concentrations of TRS than any of the freshwater Yuba River/Humbug Creek materials tested in the current study. Although TRS concentration was not measured on the deep core material used in the Alviso Slough study, TRS measurements from similar South SFB surface sediment (0–4-cm interval) locations ranged from 2.1 to 5.5 mg/g dry weight (Topping and others, 2004), which were much greater than the range of pre-slurry sediment concentrations associated with the current study (0.005 to 0.36 mg/g dry weight, table 5). In fact, the actual TRS concentration for the deep core material used in the Alviso Slough study is likely greater than the range given above for South SFB surface sediment, because the quantity of reduced sulfur minerals typically increases with depth in estuarine sediment (Marvin-DiPasquale and Capone, 1998). Thus, the material from the SYR study was much less chemically reduced to begin with (compared to the Alviso Slough sediment) and only exhibited a moderate response to the oxidizing capacity of the oxic treatment. Whereas in the Alviso case, a large amount of TRS initially present was presumably chemically oxidized under oxic conditions, and a much more pronounced affect was seen with respect to changes in Hg(II)$_R$ concentration. The important implication from this set of observations is that the predicted increases in the $\%Hg(II)_R$ associated with suspended particles from the remobilization of freshwater sediment (typically low in TRS) will be less dramatic than the predicted increase in $\%Hg(II)_R$ associated with suspended particles from the remobilization of estuarine (more saline) sediment (typically higher in TRS), because the extent of TRS reoxidation in oxidized surface water is likely to be greater in the latter case.

One interesting observation along these lines is the comparison of the Part A slurry time series of the <63 μm BRC-P2 sediment fraction associated with Experiment #2 (fig. 4) and Experiment #3 (fig. 5). In the first case, the sediment was pre-incubated at room temperature for 28 days prior to preparing the slurry; in the second case, the pre-incubation time was only 1 day. The purpose of pre-incubating the pre-slurry sediment at room temperature was to ensure reducing conditions and drive down the initial $Hg(II)_R$ concentration, according to the previous observations and hypothesis regarding the relation between $Hg(II)_R$ and reducing conditions (for example, TRS), as discussed above. For Experiment #2, the pre-slurry sediment $Hg(II)_R$ concentration was 896 ng/g (table 3), the initial $Hg(II)_R$ slurry concentration (Day=0) was approximately 175–200 ng/L (fig. 4) for the duplicate oxic slurry flasks, and the temporal trend showed a measurable increase in $Hg(II)_R$ over the first 3 days (to a maximum of approximately 400 ng/L), followed by a modest decrease over the remainder of the time course. In contrast, the same material used in Experiment #3 had a pre-slurry average sediment $Hg(II)_R$ concentration of 2,530 ng/g (table 4), and an initial $Hg(II)_R$ slurry concentration (Day=0) of approximately 450 ng/L for the single oxic slurry flask (fig. 5); no strong temporal trend was observed over the time course. While this comparison was not an exhaustive test of the effect of pre-incubation time on pre-slurry sediment $Hg(II)_R$ concentration, the longer pre-incubation time associated with Experiment #2 samples did seem to result in lower initial $Hg(II)_R$ slurry concentrations both in the pre-slurry sediment and the Day=0 slurry sample, which is consistent with the hypothesis that more reducing sediment conditions are associated with lower $Hg(II)_R$ concentrations and that when such sediments are mixed with oxygenated overlying water a notable increase in $Hg(II)_R$ concentration results.

Mercury Speciation in Pre-Slurry and Post-Slurry Solids

Although not statistically significant in all cases, there was a fairly consistent apparent loss of THg between the pre-slurry sediment and the post-slurry recovered solids in the Part A experiments (11–43% across all experiments and treatments) (tables 3 and 4). This was largely attributed to the loss of THg associated with very fine (clay size) particles in the supernatant after centrifugation to recover the post-slurry solids. Previous studies have shown that, on a dry-weight basis, sediment associated with historical Au-mine wastes generally have greater THg concentrations in fine-grained fractions (silt and clay, <63 μm) relative to sand and gravel size fractions (Ashley and others, 2002; Hunerlach and others, 2004; Alpers and others, 2006; Ashley and Rytuba, 2008; Fleck and others, 2011). Additional evidence from the venturi pump-tank experiment at the SYR-HC confluence indicates that the THg content of suspended sediment increased as particle size decreased during settling (Fleck and others, 2011). This may be due to the increased surface area-to-volume ratio of smaller particles. Thus, a loss of some percentage of these very fine particles results in a disproportionate loss of THg (and likely $Hg(II)_R$ as well) on a dry-weight basis. Because this loss mechanism only explained an average of 81±29% of the observed decrease in THg concentration between pre-slurry sediment and post-slurry recovered solids across all treatments in Experiment #3, the possibility cannot be excluded that at least some of the observed THg loss was due to either the volatile loss of dissolved gaseous Hg(0) during the week-long slurry experiment or sampling bias (for example, disproportionately sampling the smaller-size fraction of particles during the collection of the Hg(II)$_R$ time point samples). However, as detailed below, additional observations and measurements suggest that these two loss mechanisms were likely not responsible for a majority of the change in THg observed between the pre-slurry sediment and the post-slurry recovered solids.

Data from the oven-drying experiment refutes the argument that THg was lost because of Hg(0) volatilization. There was no change in THg concentrations pre- versus post-oven drying (fig. 11A), suggesting that to the extent there was liquid Hg(0) in these samples, it was not volatilized by extended heating and drying. Higher rates of gaseous Hg(0) release from liquid Hg(0) would be expected at higher temperatures. Thus, the fact that the oven-drying experiment was conducted at 70°C and the slurry experiment was conducted at room temperature (ca. 20°C) suggests that to the extent that it occurred, the temperature driven conversion of liquid Hg(0) to gaseous Hg(0) did not account for a substantial loss of THg from the slurry flasks. Further, multiple tests of pre-slurry sediment confirmed that very little (<0.02 to 3%) of the THg measured as Hg(II)$_R$ was actually dissolved gaseous Hg(0), at least during the standard 15-minute purge associated with the Hg(II)$_R$ assay. These two lines of evidence suggest that it is unlikely that an appreciable loss of THg from the slurry flasks was caused by Hg(0) volatilization. However, the sequential extraction data do suggest that a substantial amount (41–72%) of the THg pool is in the F4 fraction (table 6), which is likely associated with liquid Hg(0) (table 2). Because Hg$_2$Cl$_2$ and possibly Hg-Au amalgam are also associated with the F4 fraction (table 2), the possibility that some percentage of the F4 fraction is actually in forms other than Hg(0) cannot be ruled out. This conclusion also does not preclude minor losses of volatile dissolved gaseous Hg(0), associated with the degassing of liquid Hg(0) that may have been in the original sample, or Hg(0) formed from the abiotic (Allard and Arsenie, 1991) or microbial (Wiatrowski and others, 2006) reduction of Hg(II) during the week-long mobilization simulation.

An alternative explanation for the notable decrease in THg between pre-slurry sediment and recovered solids is slurry sampling bias associated with the under-sampling of denser heavier particles and the over-sampling of finer particles disproportionately enriched in Hg during the time course. While some degree of sampling bias cannot be ruled out completely, this explanation is largely rejected on the basis of mass-balance calculations conducted using Fe-speciation data associated with Experiment #3. Iron mass balance is helpful in understanding possible grain-size bias in sampling because a large proportion of the Fe tends to occur in mineral phases with very small particle size (for example, <63 µm). Thus, if there were a grain-size bias in the sampling of the slurry, it should be reflected in a poor Fe mass balance. Knowing the pre-slurry sediment Fe-species concentrations (table 5), the mass of sediment added to each flask, and the precise volume of filtered river water in each flask, the initial concentration of each Fe-species (Fe(II)$_{AE}$, Fe(III)$_a$, and Fe(III)$_c$) in the slurry was calculated (in units of milligrams per liter) for each flask. These calculated values were then compared to the measured Fe-species concentrations in the slurry at the beginning (Day=0) and end (Day=6) of Experiment #3 (fig. 8). When Fe$_T$ concentrations were compared between those calculated on the basis of pre-slurry sediment (Fe$_T$ = Fe(II)$_{AE}$ + Fe(III)$_a$ + Fe(III)$_c$) and those measured in the slurry at the beginning and end of the experiment ($Fe_T = Fe(II)_{AE} + Fe(III)_a + Fe(III)_c +$ magnetic-Fe), the mass balance agreed very well. Specifically, the calculated initial Fe_T versus the measured Fe_T for Day=0 agreed within -3.0 to 7.3% for all six flasks (average $\pm$ standard error, 0.5$\pm$1.6%). Further, the calculated initial Fe_T on Day=0 compared to the measured Fe_T for Day=6 agreed within -5.9 to 5.4% for all six flasks (average $\pm$ standard error, -1.3$\pm$1.6%). Thus, once the magnetic-Fe was accounted for, the Fe mass-balance calculation suggested that there was little to no sampling bias, because the calculated Fe_T concentrations effectively matched the measured Fe_T concentrations.

The argument that most of the observed decrease in THg between pre-slurry sediment and post-slurry recovered solids was associated with losses to the supernatant during the recovery of the post-slurry solids can also explain the observed decreases in $Hg(II)_R$ concentration in the pre- vs post-slurry solids (with the exception of Experiment #1). However, unlike pre- and post-slurry THg concentrations, the decreasing trend in $Hg(II)_R$ concentrations was more pronounced under anoxic conditions, compared to oxic conditions (for example, Experiment #2, Experiment #3 SYR-P1 and BRC-P2; tables 3 and 4). This may reflect the disproportional binding of larger fraction of the total Hg(II) pool to TRS or particulate organics under anoxic conditions.

The one exception to the above trend in $Hg(II)_R$ concentration was the 63–250 μm BRC-P2 material tested in Experiment #1A, which exhibited a marked increase in both $Hg(II)_R$ concentration and %$Hg(II)_R$ in the post-slurry recovered material relative to the pre-slurry sediment (table 3). One potential explanation is enhanced oxidation of Hg(0) associated with the physical breakdown of larger beads of Hg(0), facilitated by the constant mixing action and collision with other large mineral particles (for example, fine sand). Another possibility is a net decrease in the solid-phase TRS pool from the beginning to the end of the mobilization simulation experiment. However, because TRS characterization was not performed on this material, it is difficult to precisely determine what drove this trend. Clearly, the fine sand fraction (63–250 μm) behaved very differently than the silt-clay (<63 μm) size fraction derived from the same BRC-P2 zone.

Experiment #3, Part C (sequential extraction), data indicate that an extremely small percentage of THg associated with the <63 μm materials tested was water soluble Hg (F1 fraction) or weak acid (pH 2) extractable (F2 fraction); both were $\leq$0.1% of THg (table 6). In contrast, the %$Hg(II)_R$ measured in both pre-slurry sediment and post-slurry recovered solids ranged from 0.7–77% of THg (tables 3 and 4), a range much higher than can be accounted for by the F1 and F2 fractions alone. In addition to organic mercury, the F3 fraction also quantifies inorganic Hg(II) associated with particle surfaces (table 2), potentially bound to organic coatings on mineral surfaces. Thus, the $Hg(II)_R$ metric is measuring some of the same Hg(II) as is seen with the F3 fraction of the sequential extraction. This coincides with findings from previous experiments (Marvin-DiPasquale, unpublished data) that suggest much of the $Hg(II)_R$ measured is associated with Hg(II) weakly bound to the surfaces of particles. While most of the F4 fraction in the Yuba material tested is likely associated with solid-phase micrometer-sized Hg(0) and possibly some Hg-Au amalgam, very little of this is measured by the $Hg(II)_R$ assay, as discussed above. Further, the F5 fraction is the most recalcitrant and generally reflects Hg-Au amalgam and cinnabar (HgS). Apart from the latter being presumably very scarce in the SYR-HC material, because purified Hg(0) was used at this site, both HgAu and HgS are much too stable to be captured in the weak acid conditions (0.5% HCl) associated with the

Hg(II)$_R$ assay. These results suggest that a majority of the Hg(II)$_R$ measured was associated with particulate bound Hg(II).

The production of MeHg associated with the HMD-CF material during the Experiment #3, Part A, mobilization simulation (fig. 6) is likely attributable to active microbial Hg(II)-methylation. The TRS slurry concentration data are consistent with this conclusion, because TRS typically increased from the beginning to the end of the experiment (fig. 7), which is indicative of active microbial sulfate reduction. This increase in TRS over time was observed even in the aerated (oxic) treatment flasks. Although this was somewhat unexpected, the activity of anaerobic sulfate-reducing bacteria associated with the reduced microzones of particles suspended in oxic bulk media has been well documented (for example, Jørgensen, 1977). These results suggest the possibility of microbial MeHg production in an oxic water column during conditions of sediment mobilization in natural systems.

It is unclear why MeHg production was only observed for the HMD-CF material in Experiment #3, Part A, and not for the SYR-P1 or BRC-P2 materials (fig. 4), although a number of possibilities exist. The first possibility is that the MeHg produced in the case of the HMD-CF material was facilitated by abiotic reactions associated with sediment humic material (Weber, 1993) and (or) acetate (Gårdfeldt and others, 2003), which may have been minimal in the other two sediment materials tested. However, sediment humic or acetate concentration data are not available to either support or refute this suggestion, and the overall sediment organic content (measured as %LOI) was highest in the SYR-P1 material, not the HMD-CF material (table 5). A second possibility is that site-specific differences in Hg(II)$_R$ and (or) THg concentration led to the observed differences seen for MeHg production in Experiment #3, Part A. For SYR-P1, the initial pre-slurry sediment Hg(II)$_R$ concentration was 13-fold and 550-fold lower than for HMD-CF and BRC-P2, respectively (table 3). Thus, there likely was not enough bioavailable Hg(II) to drive substantial MeHg production in this case. This result is similar to that seen for these materials in the Part B (sediment mixing) experiments. In contrast, the elevated THg concentration associated with the BRC-P2 material (>9.1 ppm in pre-slurry sediment, table 4) may have inhibited MeHg production, because this concentration approached the 15 ppm level previously reported to inhibit the Hg(II)-methylating bacterial population in sediment from the Carson River Superfund site (Chen and others, 1996). Such an inhibitory effect would have been mitigated in the Part B sediment mixing experiments, because the ratio of spiking-to-receiving sediment was 1:50. Further, the HMD-CF pre-slurry sediment THg concentration (1.4 ppm, table 4) was an order of magnitude lower than the 15 ppm concentration previously reported to inhibit MeHg production in the Carson River study.

Potential for Methylmercury Production in Downstream Environments

The focus of the Part B sediment mixing experiments was to examine whether Hg-contaminated sediment mobilized from a site affected by Au mining could stimulate MeHg production in downstream depositional environments, such as river streambed sediment, reservoirs, and (or) wetland habitats. Results from three separate mixing experiments, using five different 'spiking' and 'receiving' sediment combinations, clearly demonstrates that MeHg production is possible in some situations but was dependent on both the spiking and receiving sediment tested.

The observation that BRC-P2 material did not stimulate MeHg production when the receiving sediment was either <1 mm SYR-MC bed sediment (Experiment #1, table 1, fig. 9) or <63 µm SYR-P1 material (Experiment #2, table 1, fig. 10) suggests that SYR main-channel depositional zones are not very conducive for MeHg production. In contrast, both reservoir (ENG) and wetland (DMW) receiving sediment did show a capacity for MeHg production when the spiking material was either <63 µm BRC-P2 or <63 µm HMD-CF (Experiment #3, table 1, fig. 10). Because organic matter availability is a primary factor that controls microbial rates (Marvin-DiPasquale and Capone, 1998), these results are at least partially linked to the fact that both ENG and DMW sediment had higher organic content (8.4 and 11.9% LOI, respectively; table 7), compared to both the SYR-MC material (0.8% LOI, measured) and the SYR-P1 material (6.5% LOI, table 5). This conclusion is further supported by the fact that the amount of MeHg produced in Experiment #3, Part B, was higher in the case of DMW 'receiving' sediment, compared to ENG sediment (fig. 10), with the former not only having the higher organic content (table 7), but also the higher microbial ^{200}Hg(II)-methylation rate constant (k_{meth}) and calculated MPP rate (table 7).

Table 7. Characterization of Experiment #3, Part B, receiving sediment from Englebright Lake and Delta Meadows wetland.

[The error associated with each value is given in ( ) and is based on multiple replicates (n=2–4) as appropriate. When no error term is given, n=1. **Abbreviations:** THg, total mercury; Hg(II)$_R$, inorganic reactive mercury; MeHg, methylmercury; k_{meth}, methylation rate constant; MPP, methylmercury production potential rate; LOI, loss on ignition; TRS, total reduced sulfur; Fe(II)$_{AE}$, acid extractable ferrous iron; Fe(III)$_a$, amorphous ferric iron; Fe(III)$_c$, crystalline ferric iron; Fe$_T$, total iron measured (Fe(II)$_{AE}$ + Fe(III)$_a$ + Fe(III)$_c$); E$_h$, oxidation-reduction potential corrected for the hydrogen half-reaction; ng/g dry wt, nanogram per gram dry weight; %, percent; d, day; pg/g dry wt/d, picograms per gram dry weight per day; mg/g dry wt, milligram per gram dry weight; % <63 µm, percent less than 63 micrometers; g/cm^3, gram per cubic centimeter; mV, millivolt; <, less than]

Parameter	Units	Englebright Lake		Delta Meadows wetland	
THg	ng/g dry wt	205	(10)	226	(3)
Hg(II)$_R$	ng/g dry wt	0.67	(0.03)	0.84	(0.02)
%Hg(II)$_R$	% of THg	0.33	(0.02)	0.37	(0.01)
MeHg	ng/g dry wt	2.04	(0.28)	3.25	(0.30)
%MeHg	% of THg	1.00	(0.14)	1.44	(0.13)
k_{meth}	1/d	0.104	(0.017)	0.112	(0.004)
MPP	pg/g dry wt/d	65.8	(11.0)	89.0	(3.4)
LOI	%	8.4	(0.1)	11.9	(0.1)
TRS	mg/g dry wt	0.16	(0.01)	0.26	(0.02)
Fe(II)$_{AE}$	mg/g dry wt	10.0	(0.1)	12.0	(0.5)
Fe(III)$_a$	mg/g dry wt	<0.05		<0.05	
Fe(III)$_c$	mg/g dry wt	12.1	(0.1)	2.8	(0.3)
Fe$_T$	mg/g dry wt	22.1	(1.0)	14.8	(1.1)
grain size	% <63 µm	95.7	(0.7)	78.9	(0.4)
dry weight	%	40.6	(1.3)	25.3	(0.0)
bulk density	g/cm^3	1.30	(0.02)	1.14	(0.00)
pH	pH units	6.74		6.58	
E$_h$	mV	+12		+36	

The absolute $Hg(II)_R$ concentration associated with the 0.1 g SYR-P1 spiking sediment amendment (0.17 ± 0.01 ng per 0.1 g wet weight) was 3.5-fold to >700-fold less than the $Hg(II)_R$ spiking concentration associated with the HMD-CF (0.59 ± 0.02 ng per 0.1 g wet weight) and BRC-P2 (120 ± 4 ng per 0.1 g wet weight) materials, respectively. This is most likely the reason that no statistically significant MeHg production was detected in the case when SYR-P1 was used as the spiking material (fig. 9). Specifically, if the percentage of $Hg(II)_R$ converted to MeHg was approximately the same for all three spiking materials (that is, 2–4%), then the absolute amount of MeHg formed over the 6-day sediment mixing experiment in the case of SYR-P1 would have been on the order of 0.003–0.007 ng MeHg. This concentration is below what can reasonably be detected as a change between Day=0 and Day=6 given the initial SYR-P1 plus receiving sediment MeHg concentration on Day=0 of 2.27 ± 0.14 ng MeHg per g dry weight. Thus, MeHg production associated with the SYR-P1 spike to ENG and (or) DMW receiving sediment may have occurred at levels that were below the detection limit of the experiment. Conversely, the above consideration of absolute MeHg production implies that the spike-to-receiving sediment mixing ratio may not matter much in a real-world sediment mobilization/deposition scenario, because the $Hg(II)_R$ that is converted to MeHg is ultimately associated with particles. Thus, whether those particles are ultimately mixed 1:50 with receiving sediment (as in Experiment 3) or spread out over many kilometers of similar receiving sediment, the percentage of the particle-associated $Hg(II)_R$ that gets converted to MeHg is likely to be similar. Hence, if 10 g of $Hg(II)_R$ gets mobilized and is ultimately redeposited in a region similar to DMW, but over many square kilometers, then approximately 2 to 4% of that $Hg(II)_R$ would be converted to MeHg (that is, 0.2 to 0.4 g of MeHg would be produced) over 6 days.

One of the most surprising and important results from the Part B sediment mixing experiments is the evidence for rapid abiotic MeHg production. For both HMD-CF and BRC-P2 spiking material, the MeHg concentration on Day=0 was greater than in the non-spiked control (figs. 10A and 10B). Mixing calculations indicated that this increase was not derived from the trace amount of MeHg contributed by the spiking material itself. Spike-amended Day=0 samples were frozen within 30–60 minutes after the spiking material was added (the time required to process samples in the glove bag). This comparatively short time period, relative to the week-long incubation, suggests that the observed rapid measurable increase in MeHg was not associated with microbial Hg(II)-methylation, which typically requires several hours of incubation if a Hg(II) tracer is used (for example, Hintelmann and others, 2000; Marvin-DiPasquale and Agee, 2003;) or several days of incubation without a Hg tracer (Bloom and Preus, 2003; Harmon and others, 2007). A number of abiotic MeHg production mechanisms have been proposed in the literature, including those facilitated by humic material (Weber, 1993), acetate (Gårdfeldt and others, 2003), and light (Ribeiro Guevara and others, 2008). More recently, experiments with [200]Hg(II) stable isotope amendments and killed control (flash frozen) samples indicate that the degree of abiotic MeHg formation is positively correlated with sediment organic content (Marvin-DiPasquale, unpublished data). The results presented in this report are consistent with this finding in that the more organic-rich DMW receiving sediment exhibited a higher degree of apparent abiotic MeHg formation than the less organic-rich ENG receiving sediment (table 7, fig. 10). The important point here is that the current experiments demonstrate the potential for rapid abiotic MeHg formation when sediment that contains an elevated amount of $Hg(II)_R$ is mobilized.

Can Contemporary Suction-Dredging Technology Provide a Viable Approach to Cleaning up Mercury-Contaminated Locations?

The data presented in this report provide a scientific basis for evaluating some of the potential advantages and disadvantages of suction dredging as a method for cleaning up Hg-contaminated locations. However, it is important to note that the actual efficiencies of various types of suction dredges to quantitatively remove Hg(0) and Hg-Au amalgam from sediment is a question that can only be addressed in the context of a mass-balance field experiment. A key concept in this discussion is that there are at least two distinct pools of Hg that need to be considered. The first pool is liquid Hg(0) and Hg-Au amalgam, both of which are quite dense (in the range of 13–15 g/cm^3). At some nominally large grain size (perhaps fine sand or coarse silt), Hg(0) and Hg-Au amalgam are certainly retained in a typical sluice box as evidenced by visual inspection during the field characterization part of this study (Fleck and others, 2011) and by verbal and written observations from the community of recreational suction dredgers (*http://www.swrcb.ca.gov/water_issues/programs/cwa401/docs/suctiondredge/comments/*, accessed June 1, 2010). The second pool of Hg that must be considered is Hg(II) associated with fine particles of typical grain density less than 3.0 g/cm^3 (fine sand [125–250 μm], very fine sand [63–125 μm], and silt, clay, and colloids [<63 μm]) and fine, Hg-rich particles of high grain density (for example, <250 μm) of Hg(0) and Hg-Au amalgam that may not be trapped in the typical sluice box. Thus, while a typical suction dredge may be very effective at trapping Hg from sediment associated with the first pool, it is this second pool of Hg that is of more concern with respect to long-range Hg mobilization and downstream MeHg production. This stems from the fact that it is the particle-associated Hg(II) fraction that is readily available for Hg(II)-methylation and (or) partitioning into the aqueous phase. Further, it is the 'fine' to 'very fine' sand (63–250 μm) size fraction that appears to most readily generate an increased amount of $Hg(II)_R$ when sediment is remobilized, as indicated by the results of Experiment #1, Part A (table 3). This latter observation likely stems from the fact that liquid Hg(0) particles associated with the fine-sand size class have a very high surface-area-to-volume ratio, which make them particularly prone to chemical oxidation in which mercuric oxide (HgO) forms on the particle surface during physical perturbation or breakdown (for example, flowering) (Humphreys, 2005).

It is difficult with the current data set to calculate and directly compare the relative amount of THg associated with the above two fractions (that is, large particles (>250 μm) of Hg(0) and HgAu likely to be trapped by a typical sluice box, compared to small particles (<250 μm) comprised of fine-grained Hg(0) and HgAu, as well as Hg(II) adsorbed to fine-grained mineral surfaces, less likely to be trapped by a typical sluice box). The first challenge arises from the fact that there are no data on what percentage of the total fine-grained Hg-enriched particles was retained by the sluice box. It is clear from the October 2007 dredge test that some fine-grained material was indeed trapped in the sluice box, and that the smallest size fraction (0.3–63 μm) was elevated in THg up to 14 ppm (see fig. 20 in Fleck and others, 2011). However, it was also readily apparent that the total mass of fine-grained material retained in the sluice box was small compared to the very large mass of fine-grained material in the 5–250 μm fraction that comprised the downstream plume of suspended material (see figs. 3, 15, and 16 in Fleck and others, 2011). The second challenge arises from the fact that the distribution of the larger (>250 μm) particles of

Hg(0) and Hg-Au amalgam is extremely heterogeneous in the environment in and around the SYR-HC confluence study area. Because of their high density, these particles exist largely in discrete cracks and crevices, and their distribution and thus their mass per unit volume of sediment material is not well known for the three sediment zones sampled and used in the current suite of laboratory studies (that is, SYR-P1, HMD-CF, and BRC-P2). In contrast, the distribution of the fine-grained particles (<250 μm) that are generally not trapped in a sluice box is both known and their THg concentration comparatively homogeneous, as indicated by the small %RDEV associated with replicate analyses of THg in the pre-slurry samples used in the laboratory experiments (that is, 2–8%, as calculated from tables 3 and 4). Given these facts, the amount of THg associated with <250 μm particles in one cubic meter (1 m^3) of sediment, for the three sediment types used in the current laboratory experiments (SYR-P1, HMD-CF, and BRC-P2), could be calculated. The initial assumptions:

(1) All sediment is less than ¼ in. (6.35 mm, 6,350 μm),

(2) Dry sediment density is 2.6 g/cm^3,

(3) The percentage of < ¼ in. sediment that is in the 63–250 μm and <63 μm size fractions is as calculated from the data given in table 2 of Fleck and others (2011), and

(4) The THg concentration associated with the 63–250 μm and <63 μm sediment material is as reported in table 6A of Fleck and others (2011).

Given these assumptions, the amount of THg in the <250 μm size fraction is (in units of mg THg per m^3 of <¼ inch sediment mobilized):

(1) 2.37±0.22 for SYR-P1,

(2) 131±10 for HMD-CF, and

(3) 1,560±40 for BRC-P2.

Thus, the amount of THg associated with fine particles (<250 μm), which are most likely to be naturally eroded or jettisoned out of the back of a sluice box and transported downstream, varies greatly (over 650-fold for the above three substrates) depending on the sediment compartment. The large difference in the THg concentration associated with these fine particles may be reflective of the differences in the chemical composition of the Hg species associated with them. The sequential extraction analysis of the three Experiment #3, Part A, materials (all <63 μm) indicated that the BRC-P2 material had higher proportions and absolute concentrations of Hg in the extraction fractions nominally associated with Hg(0) (F4 fraction) and Hg-Au amalgam (F5 fraction), compared to SYR-P1 and HMD-CF material (tables 2 and 6). Thus, these results suggest that, for the type of material targeted by suction dredging activity (such as BRC-P2 associated with hydraulic mining-era sediment), the very fine-grained particles can contain an elevated amount of Hg, potentially including micrometer-size (all <63 μm) particles of Hg(0) and (or) Hg-Au amalgam, that typically are not being trapped in the sluice box but are being transported downstream instead. Therefore, the use of conventional suction dredging as a method for cleaning up Hg-contaminated sediment may be potentially effective for removing the visible (sand sized and larger) particles of

Hg(0) and HgAu; however, this approach is likely to simultaneously mobilize Hg(II) associated with silts and clays that have been shown in this study to facilitate MeHg production in some downstream environments.

Acknowledgments

The authors gratefully acknowledge funding support from both BLM and SWRCB and specifically the efforts of David Lawler (BLM) and Richard Humphreys (SWRCB). We are also indebted to the numerous individuals who assisted with field work during the original collection of the samples used in the laboratory experiment, including: John Rapphahn (BLM); Matthew Wetter and Vladimir Prilepin (TetraTech); David McCracken and staff (Pro-Mack Mining); Frank Anderson, Will Kerlin, Jim Orlando, Gail Wheeler, and Elizabeth Beaulieu (U.S. Geological Survey, Sacramento, California).

References Cited

Allard, B., and Arsenie, I., 1991, Abiotic reduction of mercury by humic substances in aquatic system—An Important process for the mercury cycle: Water Air and Soil Pollution, v. 56, p. 457–464.

Alpers, C.N., Hunerlach, M.P., Marvin-DiPasquale, M.C., Antweiler, R.C., Lasorsa, B.K., De Wild, J.F., and Snyder, N.P., 2006, Geochemical data for mercury, methylmercury, and other constituents in sediments from Englebright Lake, California, 2002: U.S. Geological Survey Data Series 151, 95 p. (*http://pubs.usgs.gov/ds/2006/151/*)

Alpers, C.N., Hunerlach, M.P., May, J.T., and Hothem, R.L., 2005, Mercury contamination from historical gold mining in California: U.S. Geological Survey Fact Sheet 2005–3014, 6 p. (*http://pubs.usgs.gov/fs/2005/3014/*)

Ashley, R.P., and Rytuba, J.J., 2008, Mercury geochemistry of gold placer tailings, sediments, bedrock, and waters in the lower Clear Creek area, Shasta County, California—Report of investigations, 2001–2003: U.S. Geological Survey Open-File Report 2008–1122, 65 p. (*http://pubs.usgs.gov/of/2008/1122/*)

Ashley, R.P., Rytuba, J.J., Rogers, Ronald, Kotlyar, B.B., and Lawler, David, 2002, Preliminary report on mercury geochemistry of placer gold dredge tailings, sediments, bedrock, and waters in the Clear Creek Restoration Area, Shasta County, California: U.S. Geological Survey Open-File Report 02–401, 47 p. (*http://geopubs.wr.usgs.gov/open-file/of02-401/*)

Bloom, Nicolas, 1989, Determination of picogram levels of methylmercury by aqueous phase ethylation, followed by cryogenic gas chromatography with cold vapour atomic fluorescence detection: Canadian Journal of Fisheries and Aquatic Sciences, v. 46, p. 1131–1140.

Bloom, Nicholas, and Preus, Eve, 2003, Anoxic sediment incubations to assess the methylation potential of mercury contaminated soils, in Proceedings of the 2nd International Symposium on Contaminated Sediments: Venice, Italy, September 30–October 3, 2003, p. 331–336.

Bloom, N.S., Preus, Eve, Katon, Jodie, and Hiltner, Misti, 2003, Selective extractions to assess the biogeochemically relevant fractionation of inorganic mercury in sediments and soils: Analytical Chimica Acta, v. 479, no. 2, p. 233–248.

Chen, Y., Bonzongo, J.C., and Miller, G.C., 1996, Levels of methylmercury and controlling factors in surface sediments of the Carson River system, Nevada: Environmental Pollution, v. 92, no. 3, p. 281–287.

Cline, J.D., 1969, Spectrophotometric determination of hydrogen sulfide in natural water: Limnology and Oceanography, v. 14, p. 454–458

Fleck, J.A., Alpers, C.N., Marvin-DiPasquale, M., Hothem, R.L., Wright, S.A., Ellett, K., Beaulieu, E., Agee, J.L., Kakouros, E., Kieu, L.H., Eberl, D.D., Blum, A.E. and May, J.T., 2011, The effects of sediment and mercury mobilization in the South Yuba River and Humbug Creek confluence area, Nevada County, California: Concentrations, speciation and environmental fate—Part 1: Field Studies: U.S. Geological Survey Open-File Report 2010–1325A. (*http://pubs.usgs.gov/of/2010/1325A/*)

Fossing, Henrik, and Jørgensen, B.B., 1989, Measurement of bacterial sulfate reduction in sediments: Evaluation of a single step chromium reduction method: Biogeochemistry, v. 8, no. 3, p. 205–222.

Gårdfeldt, Katarina, Munthe, John, Strömberg, Dan, and Lindqvist, Oliver, 2003, A kinetic study on the abiotic methylation of divalent mercury in the aqueous phase: The Science of the Total Environment, v. 304, p. 127–136.

Harmon, S.M., King, J.K., Gladden, J.B., Chandler, G.T., and Newman, L.A., 2007, Using sulfate-amended sediment slurry batch reactors to evaluate mercury methylation: Archives of Environmental Contamination and Toxicology, v. 52, p. 326–331.

Hintelmann, H., and Evans, R.D., 1997, Application of stable isotopes in environmental tracer studies— Measurement of monomethylmercury (CH^{3}Hg$^+$) by isotope dilution ICP-MS and detection of species transformation: Fresenius' Journal of Analytical Chemistry, v. 358, no. 3, p. 378–385.

Hintelmann, H., Evans, R.D., and Villeneuve, J.Y., 1995, Measurement of mercury methylation in sediments by using enriched stable mercury isotopes combined with methylmercury determination by gas chromatography-inductively coupled plasma mass spectrometry: Journal of Analytical Atomic Spectrometry, v. 10, p. 619–624.

Hintelmann, Holger, Keppel-Jones, Katherine, and Evans, R.D., 2000, Constants of mercury methylation and demethylation rates in sediments and comparison of tracer and ambient mercury availability: Environmental Toxicology and Chemistry, v. 19, no. 9, p. 2204–2211.

Humphreys, R., 2005, Mercury losses and recovery during a suction dredge test in the South Fork of the American River: California State Water Resources Control Board Staff Report, May 2005, 12 p. (*http://www.swrcb.ca.gov/water_issues/programs/cwa401/docs/suctiondredge/2007merc_drdg_rpt.pdf*).

Hunerlach, M.P., Alpers, C.N., Marvin-DiPasquale, Mark, Taylor, H.E., and De Wild, J.F., 2004, Geochemistry of mercury and other trace elements in fluvial trailings upstream of Daguerre Point Dam, Yuba River, California, August 2001: U.S. Geological Survey Scientific Investigations Report 2004–5165, 66 p. (*http://pubs.usgs.gov/sir/2004/5165/*).

Jørgensen, B.B., 1977, Bacterial sulfate reduction within reduced microniches of oxidized marine sediments: Marine Biology, v. 41, p. 7–17.

Marvin-DiPasquale, Mark, and Agee, J.L., 2003, Microbial mercury cycling in sediments of the San Francisco Bay-Delta: Estuaries, v. 26, no. 6, p. 1517–1528.

Marvin-DiPasquale, M.C., Agee, J., Souse, R., and Jaffe, B., 2003, Microbial cycling of mercury in contaminated pelagic and wetland sediments of San Pablo Bay, California: Environmental Geology, v. 43, no. 3, p. 260–267.

Marvin-DiPasquale, Mark, Alpers, C.N, and Fleck, J.A., 2009b, Mercury, methylmercury, and other constituents in sediment and water from seasonal and permanent wetlands in the Cache Creek Settling Basin and Yolo Bypass, Yolo County, California, 2005–06: U.S. Geological Survey Open-File Report 2009–1182, 69 p. (*http://pubs.usgs.gov/of/2009/1182/*)

Marvin-DiPasquale, M.C., and Capone, D.G., 1998, Benthic sulfate reduction along the Chesapeake Bay central channel. I. Spatial trends and controls: Marine Ecology Progress Series, v. 168, p. 213–228.

Marvin-DiPasquale, Mark, and Cox, M.H., 2007, Legacy mercury in Alviso Slough, South San Francisco Bay, California—Concentration, speciation and mobility: U.S. Geological Survey Open-File Report 2007–1240, 98 p. (*http://pubs.usgs.gov/of/2007/1240/*)

Marvin-DiPasquale, M.C., Lutz, M.A., Krabbenhoft, D.P., Aiken, G.R., Orem, W.H., Hall, B.D., DeWild, J.F., and Brigham, M.E., 2008, Total mercury, methylmercury, methylmercury production potential, and ancillary streambed-sediment and pore-water data for selected streams in Oregon, Wisconsin, and Florida, 2003–04: U.S. Geological Survey Data Series 375, 24 p. plus appendixes. (*http://pubs.usgs.gov/ds/375/*)

Marvin-DiPasquale, M., Lutz, M.A., Brigham, M.E., Krabbenhoft, D.P., Aiken, G.R., Orem, W.H., and Hall, B.D., 2009a, Mercury cycling in stream ecosystems. 2. Benthic methylmercury production and bed sediment—pore water partitioning: Environmental Science and Technology, v. 43, no. 8, p. 2726–2732.

Mount, J.F., 1995, California rivers and streams—The conflict between fluvial process and land use: Berkeley and Los Angeles, California, University of California Press, 376 p.

Olund, S.D., DeWild, J.F., Olson, M.L., and Tate, M.T., 2004, Methods for the preparation and analysis of solids and suspended solids for total mercury: U.S. Geological Survey Techniques and Methods, book 5, chap. 8A, 23 p. (*http://pubs.usgs.gov/tm/2005/tm5A8/*)

Ribeiro Guevara, Sergio, Queimaliños, C.P., del Carmen Diéquez, Maria, and Arribére, Maria, 2008, Methylmercury production in the water column of an ultraoligotrophic lake of Northern Patagonia, Argentina: Chemosphere, v. 72, no. 4, p. 578–585.

Topping, B.R., Kuwabara, J.S., Marvin-Dipasquale, M.C., Agee, J.L., Kieu, L.H., Flanders, J.R., Parchaso, Francis, Hager, S.W., Lopez, C.B., and Krabbenhoft, D.P., 2004, Sediment remobilization of mercury in South San Francisco Bay, California: U.S. Geological Survey Scientific Investigations Report 2004–5196, p. 59. (*http://pubs.usgs.gov/sir/2004/5196/*)

Weber, J.H., 1993, Review of possible paths for abiotic methylation of mercury(II) in the aquatic environment: Chemosphere, v. 26, no. 11, p. 2063–2077.

Wiatrowski, H.A., Ward, P.M., and Barkay, T., 2006, Novel reduction of mercury(II) by mercury-sensitive dissimilatory metal reducing bacteria: Environmental Science and Technology, v. 40, no. 21, p. 6690–6696.

U.S. Environmental Protection Agency, 2002, Method 1631, Revision E—Mercury in water by oxidation, purge and trap, and cold vapor atomic fluorescence spectrometry: U.S. Environmental Protection Agency, Office of Water EPA-821-R-02-019, p. 36.

Xianchao, Yu, Chandrasekhar, T.M, and Tate, K., 2005, Analysis of methylmercury in sediment and tissue by KOH/CH3OH digestion followed by aqueous phase ethylation: Florida Department of Environmental Protection (FDEP) HG-003-2.2.